Endorsements for *Unshackled Leadership* and its earlier edition, *Making Work Work*

Making Work Work *synthesizes the best thinking in cutting-edge leadership. Scott Hunter explores the outworn beliefs and attitudes that inhibit our growth in relationships, organizations, and society at large. Not only does he expose our 'stinkin' thinkin' — he also gives us the tools to fix it. A lively, empowering guide.*

— Ken Blanchard, coauthor of *The One Minute Manager* and *The Leadership Pill*™

Scott: I just completed your book, and I think it is fabulous! Extremely well written: clear, well argued, fun to read, great examples, and above all convincing and practical. You really make the case about everyone creating their own paradigm: so why not change it? You also give compelling examples and very practical methods for us to learn to listen better.

— Michael D. Coleman, Ph.D.

There are countless books about the seven steps to nirvana at work, etc. Stop searching for magical solutions. Scott Hunter's work is all that is needed. His work stands alone. He simplifies the process. This isn't rocket science. Scott lays out a practical program for making a difference that gets positive results from the start.... The program applies to life as much as work and most of us spend most of our waking hours at work. It makes sense to let go of tired old concepts of how things are supposed to be and get on with embracing life.

— John Gartland, President, Joseph Gartland, Inc.

I read your book and thoroughly enjoyed it. I was fascinated by the concept of the internal conversation. I think you are right on about that and believe that it is truly revealing and thought provoking in understanding/explaining and predicting how someone is going to think, perceive and ultimately act. The concept about starting where you want to end is also "spot on." You have a gift for telling the story and helping people to understand what you are trying to say.

> — William S. Husak, Ph.D., Director of Intercollegiate Athletics — "Building Champions," Athletics Department, Loyola Marymount University

My life has been richly blessed as a result of reading and re-reading Making Work Work. *Scott Hunter promises to guide the reader on a path to extraordinary growth and then over-delivers.... The teachings of* Making Work Work *have taught me to create a greater vision for myself and my colleagues...and guess what: it works! The first edition is in arm's reach of my computer and a frequent reference. I know all readers will be stretched and enriched upon reading this new edition of* Making Work Work.

> — Daniel S. Cornell, Attorney, Cornell Law Group, Professional Corporation

You did a nice job of taking coaching ideas and concepts often found only in personal "self-help" books and putting them into a business context. There is no doubt that the book, and obviously your ideas, could add a lot of value to organizations, including Equis. In fact, I used some of your ideas in a team meeting in one of our offices last week.

> — Ira Dym, Vice President of Operations, Equis Corporation

Making Work Work *should be re-titled* Making Life Work. *The book presents ideas that will give you profound new insights into how humans think and interact with one another. The principles and concepts presented will also equip you to forge stronger relationships in every facet of your life. Congratulations on a great work.*

— Jeff Silverman, Senior Vice President, Director of Brand Management, The Morrison Agency

Scott, I have finished your book. What I really liked and have put into practice and have seen results in are: I have learned to tune out the conversation going on in my head when someone is talking to me and I have found the exchanges to be much more rewarding. I have also started to look for the "gold" in people instead of what do they want now or why are you annoying me. I have also started to look at the world with an abundance mentality as opposed to a scarcity mentality. Your book has caused me to rethink how I interact with those around me. I had a very delightful conversation with my daughter last week and I believe it was because of the tools you have given me.

— Bryan Volk, Controller, Ryan Companies US, Inc.

Scott's book is a fantastic road map to not just better relationships but a more fulfilling life experience. The first place I used his road map was at home and my family was the beneficiary of it. Once we started to incorporate his message into our company people started to report back deeper appreciation for their colleagues. I highly recommend this book to anyone looking to build a great culture in the work place."

— Craig A. Robbins, President, Colliers International

Scott, I just finished the book and thought it was great. It brings out so many ideas and thoughts that have been hiding in my mind for years.... I want all of my direct reports to read and understand this book. While it is titled Making Work Work, most of what you say can apply to every aspect of our life, not just work. Keep writing!
— S. Dan Anderson, Executive Director, McKenna Long & Aldridge

Scott's insights into relationships both at work and at home are phenomenal. Apply the ideas outlined in this book and you will experience incredible growth in all your relationships, whether business or personal.
— Lee Pound, Writer, speaker, editor, consultant

After 35 years in business, I thought I had a pretty good grasp on people skills. This book changed all that. Definitely one of the best written books I've read.
— George Azzanni, President, Kaiser Electric Inc.

Finished your new book and thought it was great. Not only did you touch upon important work issues but the comparisons to life issues were fantastic. It all made sense to me. Your equation of how "what comes out of our mouths" paints the scene is so true. We can paint a beautiful picture with our words or create a nightmare!
— Stephen Ballas, Senior Director — Customer service, Pernod Ricard USA

Book 2 in the Making Life Work series

Unshackled Leadership

Building Businesses
Based on Faith, Trust,
Possibility and Abundance

Scott Hunter

Hunter Alliance Press
Irvine, California

Printed in the United States of America
ISBN: 978-0-9745111-1-5

For information about our coaching, retreats, programs, seminars, or workshops, contact

THE HUNTER PARTNERSHIP ALLIANCE
Irvine, California
Toll free: 877-237-0207 • Phone: 714-573-8855
Fax: 714-573-8860
Visit our company web site: www.thpalliance.com
or send us an e-mail: info@thpalliance.com

For information about booking Scott Hunter as a speaker
call the numbers above
or visit our web site: www.scotthunter.com
or send Scott an e-mail: Scott@scotthunter.com

Hunter Alliance Press

Cover design and layout by Nancy Lashley, Athena Marketing, San Pedro, California
Text design and layout by Robert Goodman, Silvercat™, San Diego, California

*I dedicated the first edition of my book to my mentor
Lew Epstein. Lew continues to live in my heart on
a daily basis and inspires me in everything I do.*

*I dedicate this new edition not only to him
but to my friend and teacher*

Robin Duncan

*Because of her, this new edition
became necessary and possible.*

Contents

Preface

I awoke one day in 1977, looked at my life, and did not like what I saw. My marriage of 15 years had come to an end; I was separated from my children; and I was in a solo law practice, struggling to keep busy, living from month to month, with not many friends. I had come face to face with what I had tried to avoid for a long time: being alone. I clearly didn't have a life that worked or that I loved.

I questioned what I should do. End it? Settle? Accept my fate? Try to do something about it?

I chose the later course. I decided that there must be something to learn about having a great life and being successful that they don't teach you in school. They certainly didn't teach it to me either in engineering school or law school. I committed myself to discovering what that "something" was. And so the journey began.

The events and circumstances that unfolded over the next 30+ years were truly miraculous. I could never have imagined them then and they are amazing to me now. I retired as a lawyer in 1984 and began a new career as a business coach.

Since then, I have coached hundreds of organizations and hundreds of thousands of people and became a master certified coach. I also started speaking publicly in 1984, joined the National Speakers Association and have since made over 1,000 public presentations. I recently received the Certified Speaking Professional designation, the standard of excellence in the speaking profession. I have participated in so many classes, programs, seminars and courses that I have lost count.

I frequently say that I have been back in school as a student for the last 30 years. I have had the opportunity to practice everything I have learned with the hundreds of thousands of people I have worked with.

This book is the culmination of that journey. It is neither theory nor hypothesis. Everything in this book has been field-tested hundreds of times. My associates in The Hunter Partnership Alliance and I have consistently been able to produce what clients say are "miraculous results," and we have a long track record of creating extraordinary organizations.

For us, having a successful company does not happen by accident. You can even predictably create an extraordinary organization. If you follow a certain formula exactly, you will have the organization of your dreams. That's what this book is about and what you will create if you follow its dictates.

The first version of this book, *Making Work Work,* received universal acclaim when it was released in 2003. Now, four years later, it's time to add some additional insights and fine tuning as the journey has continued.

Introduction

After 20+ years of working in and observing organizations of every type and size, I have noticed a theme **all** successful ones share. They have enthusiastic, confident, optimistic, appreciative and happy people who work together on behalf of a future they have all committed themselves to.

Sports is filled with many great examples of this theme. For example, when Shaquille O'Neal and Kobe Bryant of the 1999 Los Angeles Lakers were fighting with each other, the team couldn't mount a winning streak. As soon as the two star players started to work together, the rest of the team followed suit and the Lakers won three straight championships.

In another example, at the 2002 NFL Super Bowl, the New England Patriots did something I had never seen before. Rather than individual introductions, the Patriots chose to be introduced as a team. At that moment I knew the heavily favored St. Louis Rams were in trouble. The Patriots did indeed win.

The early days of NASA provide many examples. Astronauts and mission control personnel displayed incredible levels of teamwork during the early Mercury and Apollo missions. For instance, when the Apollo 13 mission experienced a mid-flight explosion, people's lives were on the line so they had better work as a team, right? Isn't your company's success just as important to you as the success of a NASA mission was to them?

Here's the problem. In most organizations, the above components of a "successful organization" simply do not exist. It is rare to find a group of people who are enthusiastic, confident, optimistic, appreciative and happy and working together on behalf of a future they have all committed themselves to.

Quite the opposite is usually true. Very few people say they love their jobs. Significant numbers of people are unhappy at work. A 2005 Gallup poll reported that only 11% of surveyed employees said they were strongly engaged at work.

Why? Is it because people don't want to be enthusiastic, confident, optimistic, appreciative and happy? Would they rather be resigned, fearful and negative? Do people not want to be part of a team? Would they rather be selfish and loners? Of course not.

After working with hundreds of companies and tens of thousands of individuals it's clear to me that people want, more than anything else, to work in an organization where their daily activities nurture them, where they can experience and express their creativity and where management supports their commitments. People want to realize their full potential, experience a sense of accomplishment, achieve personal satisfaction, attain their goals and ambitions and receive recognition and rewards for their contributions.

Unfortunately, the majority of people don't come close to realizing these goals. A recent survey reveals a startling statistic:

only six percent of American workers love their jobs. In today's culture, Monday is blue Monday; Wednesday is hump day; TGIF (Thank God It's Friday) concludes the week. People "go to work." They trade their life and a bit of their soul for a paycheck. They tolerate endless hours of meaningless work so they can have fun on the weekend and during their two-week vacation, if they get or take a vacation.

What a sad state of affairs! This mindset not only robs people of the aliveness that's possible at work, it also robs the organization they work for of the productivity and creativity that a nurturing environment makes possible.

It doesn't have to be this way. We have the power to change this situation.

We live in remarkable times. As we began the twenty-first century, technology breakthroughs occurred every day. Today, I'm not writing this book with a pencil on a tablet. I'm writing it on a portable computer as I fly across the country at 35,000 feet.

Even as everyone jumps on the rapidly evolving technology bandwagon, the quality of interpersonal relations has improved very little, if at all. Personality conflicts, power struggles, unspoken hidden agendas, misunderstandings, turnover, and not feeling appreciated or understood, rob employees of the enthusiasm they yearn for at work and negatively impact the company's bottom line.

Do you want a truly "successful organization"? More important, are you committed to developing one? If you want to be as effective with people as you are with technology and if you want to create the kind of organization you hope is possible, then read on. You will discover that the present business climate exists for only a few reasons. Together we will look at those reasons and explore what has been done and what you can do to overcome them so you can create the organization of your dreams.

Unshackled Leadership™ is a transformational fifteen-step process that enables business leaders to achieve breakthrough outcomes and extraordinary performance. These steps are clearly laid out in the following chapters. The process requires leaders to take the following actions:

1. Wake up to the fact that there is an existing paradigm.
2. Distinguish the nature and components of your internal conversation.
3. Shift your attention from yourself and your survival to others and the contribution you can make to them.
4. Get that you are the source and creator of your reality.
5. Get that happiness, satisfaction and fulfillment are choices you make.
6. Let go of your judgments about people and look for the gold in them instead.
7. Develop an appreciation of the law of cause and effect.
8. Distinguish the predominant world paradigm of fear and scarcity.
9. Take a stand for your own worth and value.
10. Eliminate complaints and gossip from your organization.
11. See why the "honeymoon stage" of our relationships ends all too soon.
12. Clean up the messes you've made in your relationships.
13. Clarify fully the way of being that results in Unshackled Leadership.
14. Define a new paradigm of being related.

15. Align everyone in your organization on a vision for the future.

Once you complete the fifteen steps, you will:

1. Become receptive to the possibility that there may be another, more powerful way for you to think.
2. Simplify your life into two diametrically opposed paths — you will have to choose.
3. Transform all of your relationships at home and at work.
4. Take responsibility for everything in your life — stop being a victim.
5. Shift from a circumstantially determined life to a chosen life of joy, happiness and satisfaction.
6. Experience an extraordinary level of intimacy with the people in your life.
7. See that your thoughts create your attitude/mood which determines your results.
8. Shift to a paradigm of faith, trust, possibility and abundance.
9. Begin to see and appreciate the magnificence in others.
10. Create an organizational mood of joy and excitement.
11. Stop withholding your disappointments and upsets and start communicating responsibly.
12. Create an opening for championship caliber teamwork.
13. Make decisions and choices consciously and wisely.
14. Create "partnership" as a fundamental way of being with others.
15. Operate consist with your vision rather than your circumstances.

Chapter 1

The Power of Paradigms

In his book *Powers of the Mind*, Adam Smith defines a paradigm as a shared set of assumptions or beliefs. What an enlightening definition! An assumption is information we take for granted. If we take a set of beliefs for granted and all share that set of beliefs, we have a paradigm. The fact that people thought the earth was flat in the 1400s is a perfect example. Since everyone took this "fact" for granted, it became the dominant paradigm of the day.

Smith adds, "A paradigm is the way we perceive the world; like water to the fish. A paradigm explains the world to us and helps us to predict its behavior. When we are in the middle of a paradigm, it is hard to imagine any other paradigm."

Smith's analogy of a paradigm being like "water to the fish" is interesting because he's suggesting that a fish doesn't know it's swimming in water. In order for a fish to know that an environment other than water exists, it would need to come out of the water. Unless that happens, the fish is as blind to the fact that it is swimming in water as the bird is to the fact that it is flying in air.

The closing sentence in Smith's definition adds the final touch to our fish/bird analogy. When you are in the middle of a paradigm, and that paradigm is all you know, it's hard to imagine any other way to think!

Another Look

In his book *An Incomplete Guide to the Future*, Willis Harmon defines a paradigm as "the basic way of perceiving, thinking, valuing and doing associated with a particular vision of reality." He adds, "A dominant paradigm is seldom, if ever, stated explicitly; it exists as unquestioned; it is a tacit understanding that is transmitted through culture and to succeeding generations through direct experience rather than being taught."

Harmon extends Smith's definition by his statement that a paradigm is the way we think given our vision of reality. Because we can't imagine life in any other way, no one questions the paradigm. It just is.

Armed with those definitions, it is clear that at all times we live in a paradigm that impacts our everyday lives. We need to understand this for several reasons. The paradigm we live in is invisible yet it's as present as the air we breathe. Because it shapes our thinking, values and actions, it literally uses our lives. It tells us what we can and cannot think, what we can and cannot do and what we will and will not believe.

For example, let's take the fifteenth century idea that the earth was flat. It's not that people in the 1400s *believed* the earth was flat. To them, the earth *was* flat. It's doubtful that one person said to another, "I believe the earth is flat. What do you believe?" The belief just was. What don't you do when the earth is flat? Sail close to the edge! Therefore people in those days didn't.

Here's an example from the early 1950s which also shows how a paradigm shapes our thinking. Back then, conventional wisdom said, "It's impossible for a human being to run a four-minute mile. You try to run that fast, your heart will explode." Wow! What don't you do when a task is impossible? Try! Was it impossible? Of course not. However, if you think it's impossible or that your heart will explode if you try, that thought, true or not, shapes your actions. When Roger Bannister finally ran a mile in under four minutes, it didn't take long for dozens of others to do the same. Today, the accomplishment is commonplace.

My favorite example of the power of a paradigm comes from the watch manufacturing industry. In 1963, Switzerland manufactured 85% of the world's watches. Five years later, that same country manufactured just 15% of the world's watches. Over 30,000 Swiss workers lost their jobs. What happened? The quartz crystal digital watch came along.

Many people mistakenly think the Japanese invented the digital watch because that's where it was first manufactured. In reality, a group of Swiss engineers invented it. When the engineers presented their invention to higher-ups in the Swiss watch industry, the executives treated it as a toy and failed to take it seriously. Why? To them, *the new device didn't fit within their paradigm.*

What happened? That year, like every other year, Switzerland hosted a watch show. People came from all over the world to see the latest watches. The Swiss inventors displayed their "toy" without any thought that it could be taken seriously.

However, when attendees from Texas Instruments and Seiko saw the "toy," they saw much more. They took the proverbial ball and ran with it. The rest is history. Thirty thousand people lost their jobs and a country lost a big chunk of its industry, all because of the power of a paradigm.

What Does This Mean?

A paradigm acts as an information filter that determines what we perceive as reality. What may be perfectly obvious to people with one paradigm may be completely invisible to people with a different paradigm.

Finally, and most important, our paradigm determines what we can and cannot accomplish. For example, if you take a piece of land measuring one hundred yards, mark off lines every ten yards, put goal posts at opposite ends, and then give everyone baseball gloves and bats, they will find it difficult to play baseball because the field isn't set up for that game.

So it is in life. It's important to understand that we live in a particular paradigm. It's neither good nor bad, neither right nor wrong. It is what it is. Yet the paradigm you and I live in today has as much impact on us as the 1400s paradigm had on the people who lived then. The current paradigm makes us be and act in a particular way. Like water to a fish, we can't even see it!

Let me ask you a question: Are you clear that you have many beliefs? By the way, a belief is a thought you repeat to yourself over and over because you think it's the truth. Have you ever asked yourself: how come I believe what I believe? Probably not. To drive home the point, *you* didn't even decide to believe almost everything you believe!

You were born into a paradigm that had an already existing set of beliefs and you bought into virtually every one of them without any thought as to their validity or usefulness. If that's not bad enough, the vast majority of what society trained you to believe either isn't the truth or isn't very useful, which is why for so many leaders, life is like looking for downtown Chicago with a street map of Detroit. It is why ninety percent of all businesses that start each year fail within the first ten years. It is why leaders often feel like they have shackles on as they attempt to lead their organizations into the future.

So neither you nor I are responsible for our world being the way it is. It was that way when we arrived and, just like everyone else, we were trained to operate in it. As we will discuss more fully as we proceed, the existing paradigm, the one we live in here and now, is *not* set up to create enthusiastic, confident, optimistic, appreciative and happy people working together on behalf of a future they have all committed themselves to. On the contrary, it's designed to create pettiness, gossip, competition, conflict, arguments and righteousness. How do I know that? Because that's precisely what we all too frequently have!

If we keep operating in the existing paradigm as we have in the past, we'll keep getting more of what we already have. Albert Einstein defined insanity as doing the same thing over and over again while thinking we'll get a different result. My preferred version of that is: insanity is *being* the same person we've always been while thinking we'll get a different result. When you think about it, we're all a little insane, aren't we?

Consider this story. A man was walking down a dark street late one evening. As he approached a lamppost, he saw a second man frantically searching for something on the ground.

Not seeing anything, the first man said to the second, "Excuse me sir, did you lose something?" The second man replied, "Yes, I lost my keys." The first man joined the search. After a time he said, "I don't see anything. Are you sure you lost them here?" The second man replied, "Actually, no. I think I lost them down the street." Bewildered, the first man asked, "Well then, why are you looking here?" The second man answered, "Because this is where the light is!"

The same thing happens in life. Even though we don't find the joy, aliveness, fun and team spirit we want at work, we keep looking for it in the same place we've always looked.

John Stuart Mill, the 19th century philosopher and political economist, said, "When society requires to be rebuilt, there is no use in attempting to rebuild it on the old plan. No great improvements in the lot of mankind are possible, until a great change takes place in the fundamental constitution of their modes of thought."

That's what you need to do as you lead your organization into the future: Initiate a great change in the fundamental constitution of your thinking. Anything less is like putting a bandage on a broken arm. It might look good but it won't get the job done. Forget the bandage solutions! It's time to understand that if we stay as we are, we'll only get more of what we've got.

Embark on a Journey of Change

From here on we will shine a beacon on the existing paradigm to remove it from the realm of the invisible. We will see it for what it is and understand how it causes us to think and act as human beings. This exercise will make it immediately apparent why our companies, and indeed our world, are in the poor shape they are in. We will then propose an alternative paradigm — another possible way of being — that will enable us to create cooperation, caring, cohesiveness, trust, respect, and most important for company leaders, satisfaction, fulfillment, harmony, creativity and productivity.

Once we do this and commit to this new way of being, everything will flow with ease. Set up the field with a diamond, bases and a pitcher's mound and it's easy to play baseball. All that's left to do is to practice the new way of being until you get good at it, which shouldn't take long if you're willing to commit yourself to it. It's time to take off the shackles and give yourself the freedom to lead your organization anywhere you want to take it and truly experience the extraordinary.

Sound too good to be true? It isn't…as long as you're willing to tell the truth and do the work, which is the biggest challenge of all. As we will discuss in Chapter Two, people don't want to change. They don't want to admit that they don't know everything. Most people want to be right. They will blame everyone else for their problems and failures. If you're willing to move beyond that, the results can be both extraordinary and amazing.

Here's the best news of all: after years of studying our nature as human beings, I'm convinced that life isn't that complicated. Most of the time we have two choices, for now I'll call them "A" and "B." There aren't many shades of gray. Two choices, A or B. As you will see, unconsciously we choose A. More accurately, it chooses us. If you take this book seriously, you'll see what both A and B are. Your job will be to learn to stay conscious and choose B. Simple, not so easy.

Summary and Unshackled Leadership Action Items

A paradigm is a shared set of assumptions and beliefs. While we don't often think about it, we live in a paradigm that was here long before we arrived. That existing paradigm is literally using our lives. As a result, we keep doing what we've been doing and being who we've been being and wonder why we keep getting the results we get.

1. Start noticing what you believe to be the "truth." Be willing to challenge your most deeply held beliefs.
2. See if what you believe is true all of the time. Do you just ignore the facts when you encounter situations which are inconsistent with your beliefs? Maybe your deeply held beliefs are just that, beliefs.
3. Ask what life would be like for you if what you believe was not the truth? Or what would life be like if just the opposite was the truth?
4. Be willing to consider the possibility that you are living in a body of beliefs that are not only not the truth, but not even useful. Your willingness to open your mind and question everything will be an enormously valuable first step on this journey.

Chapter 2

The Components of Knowledge

In today's paradigm, we "assume" that knowledge is divided into two components. The first is "what we know." Knowing information is useful because we use what we know to produce results. You probably do this all the time.

The second component is "what we know we don't know." There are many things we know we don't know. I, for example, know that I don't know much about chemistry, medicine, nuclear science and biomechanics, to name a few subjects.

Fortunately, for the most part, we're good at dealing with what we know we don't know. We find a class, a book or an expert who knows what we don't know. We take the class, read the book or ask a question so we can move what we don't know into the column of what we do know. We can then use that knowledge to produce results.

If you look at that process, you'll see that it's fundamentally closed ended. We continue until we are satisfied that we know enough to be able to produce the results we want. Then we stop.

What if a third component to knowledge existed? What if, in addition to "what we know" and "what we know we don't know," we have "what we don't know we don't know?" This category contains that which we are blind to. It exists but we can't see it either because we don't know it's there or we don't know to look for it.

For example, when you go outside on a clear, dark night and look up at the sky, what do you see? Most people answer, "stars." Suppose an astronomer joins you. The two of you spend a couple of evenings looking up at the sky. With the astronomer's guidance, you'll be able to pick out some planets, suns, moons, galaxies and satellites. Next an astrologer joins you and you spend a couple of evenings with him. Now you're able to see Virgo, Capricorn, Libra and Pisces in those mere stars.

Where were the planets, galaxies and constellations before your two experts arrived? They were always there. You just didn't have the eyes to see them.

The Great Unknown

Unfortunately, as in the last example, much exists that we can't see even though it's right under our noses, which is a frustrating predicament. After all, if we don't know that something exists, how can we formulate a question to ask about it? The answer is that we can't.

By the very nature of the current paradigm, much is invisible. What we want and what we need is there but we can't see it. The fact that it's there, using us without our knowledge or understanding creates the problems we experience, hampers our relationships and prevents us from effectively leading our teams. It's all that "stuff" we can't see that puts us in the shackles we experience.

Your goal here is not to learn more "stuff." You're already smart. Your goal is to take what lives in the unseen and bring it into the light of day. When you see what the current paradigm has hidden from you for so long, you will become more effective at accomplishing what you already have to do.

Together we will go on a journey. We will engage in a dialog about things you may not know as well as things you may not know you do not know. Your job is to go on the journey with me and look...but not for answers. You may find some answers, but those are the booby prizes, not what we're looking for. Instead of answers, we're looking for insights or "a-ha" moments. My objective is to enable you to see what you haven't seen before.

During our journey, I'll ask you to "map it onto your experience." This means I want you to think about what you just read, reflect on it and compare it with your own experiences. Discover what fits and what doesn't. Perhaps this information will explain how you experience your job on a day-to-day basis and allow you to do that job in a way you haven't experienced before or in a way that allows you to handle a tough situation more effectively.

I hope to arouse your curiosity so you keep inquiring into the subjects we'll discuss. This book is not "the answer." I'm not smart enough to give you *the* answer. I'm certainly not smart enough nor do I know enough about you to give you *your* answers. Therefore, the challenge is to give up the need for answers and be happy with the search.

The Nature of an Inquiry

Here's an example from my own life to show you how the process works. I married right out of college and for all the wrong reasons. I was leaving home for the first time and was scared to be on my own. I married someone who would keep me company on my journey into the unknown. Whether we were compatible or even whether we loved each other wasn't relevant. I just didn't want to be alone.

You've probably guessed that that relationship didn't turn out well. Fifteen years and two children later we divorced. I dated for several years but when it came to relationships I was as clueless then as I was in college. In the early '80s I gave up. I didn't know how to have a successful relationship so I stopped trying. "Love 'em and leave 'em" became my mantra.

Then in 1985, during my first job as a business coach, one of the coaches in the company asked me if I was in a relationship. I quickly gave him my standard answer: "I don't do relationships." During the conversation that ensued, he convinced me that my decision to not pursue a relationship was not useful and that it would be a lot wiser for me to learn how to have a great relationship rather than give up.

I remember saying to him, "Okay. I'm going to learn what it takes to have an extraordinary relationship with everyone in my life and with a woman in particular." Thus began the inquiry into "what I needed to know" and "whom I needed to be" to have extraordinary relationships with the people in my life.

No matter how much time passes, that inquiry never ends. Every day gives me another opportunity to discover what I don't know I don't know. While I've found many ideas that look like "answers," and they are frequently useful, the inquiry never stops. I have had many insights into the nature of human beings and the nature of relationships. I've had many "a-ha" moments and I now see many things I couldn't see before.

These insights have allowed me to experience far more satisfying relationships than I ever thought possible. When I share these insights with clients, they achieve similar results.

So don't look for answers here. I don't offer formulas, prescriptions, rules, habits or "ten steps." My job is to take you on a journey into the existing paradigm. Map what you read onto your experience. See if it fits. Try out the ideas. Be open to where they take you and be willing to "try on" what I say.

Dr. Martin Luther King, Jr. once said, "Who we are as human beings is only increasing that which we already know and which we have a reference for. We want a quick fix, an easy answer, the fast solution." Please don't be one of these "quick fix, easy answer, fast solution" people. They never get far.

Relationships will continue to be a challenge and a struggle. However, armed with the insights this book offers, you'll be on your way to having rich, meaningful, quality relationships with everyone in your organization and in your life as you provide extraordinary leadership for your team.

One last caution: After having this dialog with hundreds of thousands of people, I have found that many individuals have a difficult time relating to information they don't understand, they have not heard before, or they have no reference for. They respond in a variety of ways. Some get angry, others get defensive; some get frustrated, others resist, and the rest argue. In extreme cases, they check out. Their body is there, but they are not present.

You may have some or all of these reactions and that's okay. They're all normal and human. The important thing is that you hang in there. We're building something new, and you won't see its power and value until you get close to or arrive at the end. It's like a jigsaw puzzle. The picture doesn't become clear until most, if not all, of the pieces are in position. If you hang in there to the end and don't skip anything, I promise you the results will be nothing short of miraculous.

Declare Your Commitment

The value you get out of this book is directly related to what you're committed to get out of it. Recall the last time you flew on an airplane. As the plane taxied from the gate, the flight attendant or the TV monitor delivered the pre-flight safety instructions. What were you and most of the other passengers doing at that moment? Most likely something other than listening and watching. Hey, you've heard it all before, right? Besides, at that moment, you weren't concerned about possible trouble.

However, suppose you are flying at 30,000 feet and the plane begins to shake. Out the window you see smoke billowing from one of the engines. Just then the flight attendant announces that the pilot is going to make an emergency landing in the water. She proceeds to give you instructions on how to prepare. Do you listen to her now? You bet. Why? Because now something is at stake, namely your life. When something important is at stake, we listen in a different way. Our commitment is different.

The breakthroughs I am commited to producing as a result of my reading this book are:

Personal | Business

I remember an incident that brought this point home to me. In the late '80s, I was part of a company that was exploring what it took to coach people to produce extraordinary results. As part of our work, we staged an event with some of the day's greatest sports coaches to learn what made them great coaches. Red Auerbach, the Boston Celtics basketball team coach; John Wooden, the basketball coach from UCLA; George Allen, the football coach of the Washington Redskins; and Tim Galway, the author of *The Inner Game of Tennis*, appeared.

Our company president interviewed the four coaches in a TV studio and we broadcast the program around the country. I sold tickets and hosted a viewing in southern California where about 100 people watched the interview. At the end, we discussed what the attendees learned from the conversation.

One man eagerly leaped to his feet and said that he had been in corporate America for over thirty years, with many Fortune 500 companies, and that he had participated in innumerable programs. He thought this was the most powerful, insightful and valuable program he had ever witnessed. He couldn't wait to get to work so he could put into practice what he had learned.

Then another man stood up. He was a company CEO and a former pro football player. He said that the presentation was fun, that Red was a bit of a character, that John was very charismatic, and that George was obviously smart and intense, but that was it.

Then another man, an accountant, stood up and said that this had to be the stupidest program he had ever attended. He claimed that it was a total waste of time. He wanted his money back, which I gladly gave him as he stormed out the door.

How could three people at the exact same program have such different reactions? Simple. Each came expecting something different and each had a very different commitment.

Before you continue, please get a pen and complete the chart on the facing page.

You may be wondering exactly what constitutes a "breakthrough." In my definition it's an unprecedented or unexpected result, something you cannot predict. It is out of the ordinary, not a reasonable extension of the past. It may be something that others broadly accept as a breakthrough, or something very personal.

Now write!

What are you willing to put on the table for exploration as you read this book? What kind of commitment will you make to your business and to your personal life to produce a "breakthrough" as a result of what you will learn from this book? What relationships are not as strong as you'd like them to be? In what areas do you feel inadequate, insufficient, ineffective or frustrated as a leader? What results do you want to produce that you're not currently producing? What problems do you have that you can't solve?

When I ask people at executive retreats to do this exercise, they write remarkable things. Some statements are simple, such as, "I'd like to be able to say what's on my mind without fear of retribution." Others are as heart wrenching as, "I haven't spoken to my brother for thirty years and would like to know what to do about that." Please don't proceed without writing down what's important to you.

The comedian Flip Wilson once said, "What you lose is what you don't bet when you win." Don't make the mistake of not winning *really, really* big because you neglected to bet on what you could accomplish. In writing this book, I am committed to providing you with the insights and tools necessary for you to be an extraordinary leader, to create an extraordinary organization, and for you and all the people around you to win big. In fact, you can't lose so you might as well bet the farm. Mention everything that you would like to get out of reading this book. I promise that it's all within your reach.

Summary and Unshackled Leadership Action Items

In the existing paradigm, we operate like all information is either in the category of what we know or what we don't know. We don't realize that there is much that we are blind to, things we don't even know we don't know. This book is about uncovering and shining a beacon on these blind spots which, when seen, will allow you to be more effective in dealing with the everyday situations you confront at work.

1. Be sure to fill out the chart in this chapter and keep adding to it as you go through your week.
2. What relationships are not as strong as you would like them to be? Write them down.
3. In what areas do you feel inadequate, insufficient, ineffective or frustrated as a leader? Write them down.
4. What results do you want to produce that you're not currently producing? Write them down.
5. What problems do you have that you can't seem to solve no matter how hard you try? Write them down.

*Step 2: Distinguish the
nature and components of
your internal conversation*

Chapter 3

Choose Which "Conversation" Dominates Your Thinking

Throughout the day, from the moment you wake up to the time you fall asleep, something remarkable takes place. Whether you're showering, getting dressed, eating breakfast, driving to work, sitting at your desk, participating in a meeting, eating lunch, driving home, cooking dinner or preparing for bed — in other words, all the time — there's a conversation going on. You know the one. It's part of the internal dialog that just asked you, "What conversation is he talking about?" It's the conversation you wake up with in the morning, that's with you all day and sometimes keeps you up at night.

How do you relate to that conversation? What do you call it? Among the typical answers I get from audiences are: thinking, having thoughts, self-talk, my mother, the committee, radio Hanoi and the gremlin. It doesn't matter what you label the conversation. What matters is that you notice the conversation and realize it's there all the time. Sometimes you are in control of the conversation. More often you're not.

For example, aren't there times when you're driving in your car, sitting at your desk or flying across country and you find yourself in the middle of a conversation and you have no idea where it came from? And aren't there times when something is "on your mind" and you wish whatever it is would go away and leave you alone but it won't?

Unfortunately, most people don't pay much, if any, attention to this conversation. "Why should we?" they ask. "It's just self-talk or thinking." No... it's much more than that.

In The Beginning

Let's start with my understanding of where that conversation comes from and what it's all about.

The day we are born, for all practical purposes there is no conversation. That doesn't last for long. Events occur: our diaper is wet; we're hungry; we hear a loud noise; we're picked up; we need to burp; we cry. Sometimes someone comes to take care of us right away; other times they don't. At any given time, any one of a number of people is around us doing something. Mothers, fathers, sisters, brothers, grandparents... the list goes on and on.

Soon we grow, mature and become profoundly curious. We crawl; we walk; people react to what we do. We go to school and interact with other children and teachers. The number of events we experience is endless.

In reality, none of these events inherently mean anything. I know you likely don't believe that statement and that's okay. Human beings have a hard time believing that events don't mean anything. In fact, we believe just the opposite. We think that *everything* that happens means *something*.

So, beginning at an early age, we interpret everything that occurs and assign it a meaning. It's important to understand that for us the event does indeed have the meaning we give it, whether fact or not. For us, it is "true."

Then we store the event, with the meaning we gave it, in our consciousness. It doesn't stop there. The next event occurs; we interpret it, give it meaning and store it away. We repeat this process again and again and again. Along the way, we make judgments and decisions about ourselves, the world, other people and how we fit in. What emerges is an elaborate story about everything. The entire process — the decisions, the judgments, the story — are all a part of our conversation.

Therefore, your conversation — the one you wake up to in the morning and the one that stays with you all day and into the night — is the sum total of the process just described. Stored within you are all the events you have ever experienced with the meaning you gave them attached and all the decisions, judgments and concepts that evolved as a result of that process.

Later we will discuss some of the judgments and decisions we often make. For now, it is sufficient to say that you live in a conversation, that within that conversation is your paradigm, and that what makes you *you* is that conversation.

How it Evolves

Here's an interesting idea to consider. I have heard it so many times from so many reputable sources that I believe it is true: If I could listen to your conversation, the one that is using your life and determining who you think you are, who you think other people are, and everything else about the world you live in, I would find that 50% of your conversation today was there by the time you were five years old! I would further find that 80% of your conversation today was there by the time you were eight years old, and 95% of your conversation today was there by the time you were eighteen years old.

Now that's scary. It means that at least 80% of the time, the person doing the thinking for you is no more than an eight-year-old child. Do you know some adults who act like two-year-olds? Probably lots. That's because they're still acting out some major event that occurred when they were that age. When working with people as a coach, I find it useful to frequently remind myself that the person I am interacting with is often a five-year-old trapped in a big body. You might consider doing the same.

What can you do with this information right now? Nothing...yet. It's simply something to think about, but it's also extremely relevant to the rest of this discussion. For now, just entertain the thought that you live in a conversation, that within that conversation is your paradigm, and that what makes you *you* is that conversation.

Welcome the "ego"

Now I want to partially contradict what I just said. If you dig further into this phenomenon of "the conversation," you will discover that there are two very different conversations going on within you. I find it useful to think about it this way: we all have a split mind, many call one our upper mind and the other our lower mind.

The upper mind is the home of our "higher consciousness." Every philosopher, every religion and every great thinker, from Buddha to Jesus and many others has acknowledged the presence of our higher consciousness. This is the voice of peace, love, oneness, togetherness, possibility and harmony. Theologians call this the voice of God. Call it whatever you want.

The lower mind is the home of the ego. It is the part of our mind that was programmed as described above when I discussed the birth of "the conversation." As we will see, it is the voice of fear, limitation, separation, scarcity, greed, and much more.

For now, realize that the ego is not your friend and does not have your best interests at heart. You'll see why as we proceed. The biggest challenge you'll face as you go on this journey is: the ego always speaks loudest and always speaks first. For the majority of people, the voice of the ego is so loud they never hear the voice of their higher consciousness. Even when we are called into action by that voice, the ego fights it with all the power it has.

As I said before, I believe life is not all that complicated. In fact, at least in theory, it's simple. Always two choices, A or B. In this case, listen to the voice of the ego or listen to the voice of your higher consciousness. We'll continue to develop this theme as we proceed. Ready to proceed?

Summary and Unshackled Leadership Action Items

You live in a conversation; within that conversation is your paradigm. What makes you *you* is that conversation. Actually, two conversations are going on within you, one is the conversation of your higher consciousness; the other is the conversation of your ego.

1. Start paying attention to your inner dialog.
2. Start to notice how frequently it has a mind of its own, that it's not just thinking, that it's often a stream of thoughts you have little or no control over.
3. See if you can distinguish the conversation of your higher consciousness from that of your ego. It's pretty simple to tell which is which. The first makes you happy. The other makes you afraid.
4. If you're able to distinguish the conversation of your higher consciousness from that of your ego, see what percentage of the time you listen to each.

Chapter 4

Listening in the Existing Paradigm

Books and courses abound on "active" listening and other so-called effective listening techniques. But I ask you: have any of those ideas really made a difference? While they may have helped a little, as a "technique" they have their limitations. Let's examine listening in a new way — a way that *will* make an enormous and permanent impact on your life and your effectiveness as a leader.

To get started, have you ever had a conversation with someone and you walked away saying to yourself, "I might as well have been talking to the wall?" Are you willing to admit that at times people have conversations with you and likely walk away thinking, "I might as well have been talking to the wall?" If you're honest, I'm confident that you answered both questions with a resounding "yes." Let's take a look at why that is.

Typically we approach a conversation with another person as if they were a blank canvas upon which we can write words that they will receive and understand exactly as we intend. When they don't "get" our message exactly as we intend, we get irritated and think they must not be listening, don't understand, are playing games or being hostile.

But given everything we've said so far, are we really speaking to a blank canvas? Of course not. The other person is living in his or her conversation. Before you even open your mouth, he is already listening, to *himself.* Why? Because people are *always* listening to their own internal conversation.

In workshops and speeches, I often ask the audience, "Has anyone ever asked you: Are you listening to me?" A laugh of recognition usually follows because we've all been asked that question. I then ask, "What's the only honest answer you can give someone if she asks that?" The answer of course is, "No, I'm not listening to you; I'm listening to me listening to you!"

So the question is not *whether* we are listening when someone speaks to us. It's a question of *how* we are listening. We always have an internal conversation going on as we listen to another person and that conversation filters everything we hear. As a result of many years of looking at this subject and participating in innumerable programs, I have come to realize that virtually everyone listens in one or more of a particular set of ways. Try to identify the way *you* listen as we go through some of the more common ones.

The Disempowering Listening Filters

❧ *Get to the Point*

When I first began to pay attention to how I listened (that is, listening to my internal conversation when people spoke to me), I realized that my predominant way of listening was what I call *get to the point.* I was always busy and very much focused on what *I* was doing and the importance *I* assigned to it. In my mind, people, like secretaries, vendors, friends, children and even my spouse, were always interfering with whatever *I* happened to be doing at the moment. Couldn't they see I was busy? I wanted them to get to the point quickly so I could get back to what I was doing.

As they'd talk to me, internally I would be saying, "What's this all about? Why are you telling me this? Can't you see I'm busy? Would you please hurry up and get to the point!" In fact, it would often be so bad that if they didn't *get to the point* quickly, I would say something like, "Would you please tell me the point of all this."

Many years after the fact I realized why I had so much trouble keeping a secretary for the fifteen years I was in private law practice. Instead of treating my secretary as a valued ally, I treated her as an interruption to something more important that I had to do.

Can you relate to this way of listening? In almost every group I speak to, when I ask how many people in the audience listen *get to the point*, most of the hands go up. Perhaps this is a result of our fast-paced society, where everyone is working hard to overcome his or her fears and sense of scarcity while staying one step ahead of the bill collectors.

❧ *Agree/Disagree*

Another common way people listen is to determine if they agree or disagree with what you are saying. A variation of this is when people listen to determine whether you are speaking the truth. You'll be talking to someone and he or she will say, "Yes, I agree with that (or I believe that)," or "No,

I don't agree with that, or that, but yes, I agree with that…"
And so forth.

These people know what they know, believe what they believe, and then listen to see if what you are saying fits or doesn't fit into their existing belief system. If it does, you're obviously very wise, as wise as them, and they acknowledge you for that. If it doesn't, you're obviously ignorant or uninformed, and they let you know that. Strike any chords?

I recently had an experience with an *agree/disagree* person which would have been funny if it wasn't so sad. I was on a bicycle trip in Germany with a group of people from all around the United States. One young woman from Los Angeles could easily have been labeled a "drama queen." Every day she had another catastrophe. First she lost her passport, the next day it was her wallet, and on and on.

About five days into the trip, I saw her out walking in the town where we were staying. With the desire to help her as best I could, I approached her and asked, "Can I share something with you that I've learned that I think would make a big difference in your life?"

She smiled and replied, "Certainly, I'd love to hear what you have to say and I'll see whether I agree with it or not."

I knew in advance that I was going to share information that she didn't already know and not wanting to get into a debate with her, I said: "Well if you're only going accept what I say if you agree with it, and I suspect you won't, what's the point?"

She didn't get what I was alluding to and again repeated her desire to hear what I had to say to see if she agreed with it or not. At that point, seeing I was barking up the wrong tree, I changed the subject and walked on.

❧ *What Am I Going to Say Next?*

I have lots of relatives who listen in a way I call *what am I going to say next?* People who listen this way like (or rather, need) to do all the talking. In fact, they think that's the way you win friends and influence people. *Talk, talk more, talk a lot* is their motto. They want people to "get" how brilliant they are.

So when someone else is speaking, they're just listening to get ammunition for their next comment. When they get their cue, they typically interrupt you mid-sentence and go on their merry way. Or they wait patiently for you to stop talking so they can have their turn. Does this sound like anyone you know? Yourself maybe?

Sometimes I have to laugh at the conversations I used to have with my mom. *She'd* ask *me* a question, like how's the weather in California (where I live — she lived in Florida), and I'd start to answer. In the middle of my sentence, she'll pick up on a word I use to describe our weather (which relates to her weather), and start to tell me about the weather in Florida. It's like she never asked me a question at all. Have you ever had this happen to you, or have you ever done this to another?

One time I started to tell her about a party I went to. The moment I mentioned the word "party," she immediately interrupted me to tell me about a party she and my dad had gone to.

It got to the point with my mom that when I would call her, I would just say a word, like "weather" or "party," and let her talk. Why bother to try and finish my sentence if I know I'm not going to get the opportunity to do so.

❧ Let Me Tell You What You are About to Say

A slight variation of the previous way of listening is people who listen with the goal of *figuring out* what you're going to say next. After all, they know you, they've heard you talk before, they're sure they know where you're going with this, and to show how smart they are (or because they don't have the patience to let you finish) they finish whatever you are speaking about for you. It's like they're playing a game called *let me figure out what you are going to say and tell you.*

My massage therapist is like this. I actually find her quite amusing. If you were to observe our conversations, you would see that I get 75 to 80% of the way through each sentence before she finishes my sentence for me. It's amazing how frequently she's right on. I guess I've gotten a lot of massages from her.

❧ I'm Always Right

Some people think, and actually believe, that there is a *right* way to do *everything* and, conversely, a *wrong* way to do everything. Guess who knows the right way to do everything? You guessed it — they do! While they don't say or admit this, they do *everything* the *right* way. That's what makes it the right way; it's their way.

These folks also constantly compare what you are doing to the *right* way of doing things. As you would expect, they are very good at telling you that your way is the *wrong* way.

People who listen this way often startle me. They seem to have no perception that *everyone* has a *unique* way of functioning, that there is no *right* or *wrong* way, and that it's all a matter of opinion and preference. They truly believe there is just one way of doing everything — the right way, which is *their* way.

Shortly after I moved to a beach house in Southern California, I invited some friends and relatives over for a party. I provided some of the food and invited people to bring snacks to share as well as whatever they liked to drink. When people arrived, we put all the food, snacks, and drinks on the dining room table. I provided plates and glasses and ice. My guests helped themselves to the food and drink, allowing me to mingle and enjoy the party with everyone else.

When my sister arrived at the party, it didn't take long for her to lecture me that "you just don't do that at a party." She proceeded to explain that when "you" have a party it's "your" responsibility to provide the food and the beverages. If a guest wants to bring food, that's up to them, not you. It's also "your" responsibility to pour the drinks and make sure everyone always has whatever they need. She gave me more instructions, but I don't remember them now.

Thus started a long history of my sister explaining to me, at just about every opportunity, how things are "supposed" to be done and how inappropriate I was for doing things the "wrong" way. Do you know anybody like that?

❧ *I Need to Win*

An offshoot of *I'm always right* is when people turn every con-versation into a debate. As soon as you start a conversation with a *debate* person, you can feel the energy shift. They go on the offensive. This way of listening is not so much about being right or wrong, it's about winning. These people will argue and argue and argue and argue, until you either give up or admit that they've won.

I experienced this before the 2004 presidential campaign. A group of friends who lived in Oakland were clearly activists on behalf of one of the candidates. I happened to be in the area on business and invited them to dinner, mostly because they are dear friends and I wanted to spend time with them.

During the dinner, I asked why they were so adamantly in favor of their candidate. One of them went on a rampage. With great energy, he launched into a lengthy monologue about the virtues of that candidate and the negatives of his opponent. He ended his tirade with the statement: "I can't believe anyone with a half a brain would even think about voting for candidate ___. So who are you planning to vote for, Scott?" Seeing where this conversation was going, I changed the subject.

❧ *Attack*

I have met many people who, especially in close, intimate rela-tionships, listen as if they are being *attacked*. For whatever rea-son (the reasons for all of these ways of listening will become clear before long), they fear you are out to get them, to make them wrong, or take advantage of them. They are on guard, on the defensive. No matter what you say, they respond as if you had just attacked them.

Very often it's the most casual of comments, the slightest criticism, the off-hand remark that they rebut with a surprisingly hostile response, as if you had just intentionally stuck a knife in their heart. I'm always caught off-guard when someone responds this way. I can't imagine how they could have heard what I said in a way that prompted such a response.

❧ *Find the Flaw*

Of course, no list like this would be complete without mentioning the people who, no matter what the idea or possibility, tell you why it *won't* work. These people listen to *find the flaw.* They've seen and tried everything. They've been there, done that; they know that there is some reason why every idea won't work. It's their goal to tell you precisely what that reason is. They listen for the flaw in your plan and then leap to your rescue.

One time I worked with a retail company that had a number of branch locations. As we worked on reinventing the company and designing a powerful new future, we would frequently bring all of the branch managers together for a meeting to explain the new initiatives. One manager, no matter what we proposed, would sit with his head down, shaking it from side to side, signaling his disapproval in a not-so-subtle way.

When we completed a presentation, I would ask what he thought of the proposal. He consistently told us all the reasons why it made no sense, why it wouldn't work, and why it was tried before and failed. Interestingly enough, he sometimes came up with valid reasons why we should reconsider what we were planning so he played a very important role in the company.

❧ I Know

Some people listen *I know*. These people know everything. Just ask them! Whatever you say, they say, "I know." If you ask them how they know, they say, "I just know."

I've recently discovered I have a friend that listens this way. I seem to be learning so many new things at such a rapid rate these days and, because she is a good friend, I often share the latest and greatest "a-ha" moment with her. She always listens quietly and when I get done says something like: "Isn't it great to know that" or "I'm so happy you got that sorted out" or "I've been doing that for months now. So happy for you."

I'm actually convinced that most of the time, she has no idea what I'm talking about but that doesn't matter to someone who listens *I know*.

❧ *Either/Or*

Another common way of listening, which is usually not *instead* of but *in addition* to these other ways, is called *either/or*. This way of listening stems from childhood. Remember being told when you were young that you can't have your cake and eat it too? This message told you that life is about choices. As a result, some people believe that everything has to be one way or another, and they listen to hear the choices. They believe that sooner or later, everything comes down to a compromise or a choice.

⁕ *Are You Approving of Me?*

The final group of people listen simply to determine whether the speaker approves or disapproves of them. People who listen this way are fundamentally insecure about their own self worth. Rather than resolving that insecurity within themselves, they look to others for validation. The whole focus of their listening is to see if they are being approved of or not.

Back to You

Keeping in mind the methodology of this book, re-read the above ways that people listen. Here's the list:

- Get to the Point
- Agree/Disagree
- What Am I Going to Say Next?
- Let Me Tell You What You are About to Say
- I'm Always Right
- I Need to Win
- Attack
- Find the flaw
- I Know
- Either/Or
- Are You Approving of Me?

Map them onto your experience. Can you identify the predominant way you listen? What about the other people in your life? Your spouse, your children, your key executives and employees? Next time you speak to any of these people, or to anyone for that matter, listen to how they respond. Try to identify the way they listen. With practice, you'll be able to do this easily. This exercise will help you understand the world they live in and why they react to things the way they do.

Now that you've identified the primary way you listen, consider the possibility that at different times you listen in most if not all of the ways described above. Can you see that this is the case? It's a good idea to tell yourself the truth about how you listen.

That brings us to the next question: Do you decide in advance how you're going to listen? That is, do you decide in advance that when you walk into the office in the morning you're going to listen *agree/disagree,* and then at 10 a.m., in the sales meeting, you're going to switch to *get to the point*? Likely not, correct? Likely, you just listen how you listen without thinking about it. When I ask people at a speech or in a seminar, "How many of you decide in advance how you are going to listen?" I always get a laugh as the predominant response. Think about how I'm going to listen in advance? It seems ridiculous.

These ways of listening are unconscious and automatic. Our conversation is what it is. It has a mind of its own. We listen how we listen, we react to the things we react to without much forethought and it's just that way. The fact is, as you learned in our discussion about beliefs, you were born into a paradigm where you were trained to listen in these ways, just like everyone else, without any thought on your part whatsoever.

People are not aware of the power of their listening. We live the life of the victim, as if someone "out there" is out to get us. Let's be clear. There is no such thing as a victim. We shape our world with how we listen. If we listen *attack*, guess how everything shows up for us? Like an attack! If we listen *agree/disagree*, then that's what's available to us in any discussion. You get no new information, no new ideas, and no ability for anyone to make a difference with you. All you get to do is agree or disagree.

Do you know people who are skeptical? Consider that there is no such thing as "being skeptical." You can show me a table or a chair or a tomato, but can you show me skepticism? No. It's just a way of listening.

Skepticism is an internal conversation that goes like this: "I know that many things (maybe most things) are BS, a rip-off, not what they appear to be. This probably is too, and you can't fool me!" It's a way of listening to defend yourself against being made to look foolish.

We can have the same discussion about resignation. Can you show me resignation? No. It's a way of listening. It's a conversation that "nothing will change; this won't make a difference; it hasn't worked in the past, so it certainly won't now."

It's all unconscious. And these are the ways people listen.

The Pattern in the Process

Who do you have your attention on when you listen in *any* of the previously described ways? Obviously yourself!

The important question is: What do you think these ways of listening are designed for? In other words, if you were to design human beings and have them listen in the ways listed above, what do you think the underlying purpose would be? Please take a moment, go back over the list, and see if you can identify the design.

❦

If you did the exercise, you'll realize that in *all* of these ways of listening, you focus your attention on yourself and your only concern is your own self-interests. You are concerned with protecting yourself because each of these ways of listening is fundamentally adversarial in nature. You're over there; I'm over here. You show up as a threat to me and I have to protect myself from you.

Why can't we all get along? In most interactions, at least interactions in the existing paradigm, we have person X with his attention on himself and concerned with his own self-interests and person Y with her attention on herself and concerned with protecting herself. When they talk to each other, do they have a meaningful, intimate conversation? No way. Most conversations resemble two television sets tuned to different channels broadcasting at each other.

This is the work of the ego. The ego has only one concern: its survival. For the ego, you are the center of the universe, everyone else is separate from you and, what's worse, they are all enemies.

This is why we rarely experience true communication between people. Each person's primary concern is his or her own self-interest and desire to make sure the other person hears what he or she has to say. People place very little or no attention on making sure they understand the other person.

This is the root cause of most miscommunication and upsets between spouses, parents and children, team members, bosses and employees. It certainly is our experience in most of the companies we've worked with.

In addition to becoming conscious of your listening, you also need to understand that when you listen in any of these ways, your end-product is precisely what these ways of listening are designed for…your survival. If that's what you want, then go ahead and listen that way. Just recognize that like everything else in life, there are consequences for everything you do and every way you are.

Here are some of the consequences of having your attention on yourself and listening in one or more of the previous ways: You experience no real communication, no understanding, no appreciation of the other person's position, no intimacy and certainly no trust. These consequences cost you your satisfaction, happiness, sense of well-being, self-confidence, joy, aliveness and ultimately the relationship. In a business setting, it costs productivity, creativity, teamwork, enthusiasm, turnover, success, and of course, money, results and accomplishment. The ego is totally unconcerned that you are suffering these consequences since they are exactly what it wants.

Is it any wonder that our companies, our relationships, and our world are the way they are? Is it any wonder that communication doesn't work and that our relationships suffer? We'll talk more in Chapter 12 about why we are this way, but for now let's recognize that our listening has an impact on our relationships and our lives. We can better understand all of the ways of listening discussed in this chapter when we look at them as self-protection strategies…and the work of the ego.

Summary and Unshackled Leadership Action Items

The question is not *whether* we are listening when someone speaks to us. It's *how* we are listening. As we listen to another person, we always have an internal conversation going on that filters everything we hear. In the ordinary course of events, we have our attention on ourselves and the internal conversation is designed for our survival.

1. See if you can identify your predominant internal conversation when people are speaking to you. Does it change from situation to situation or does it have a consistent theme?
2. Then see if you can identify the listening of the people you have the most frequent contact with.
3. If you're willing to acknowledge that you have your attention on yourself and listen get to the point, what am I going to say next, agree/disagree, etc., start to notice the impact that way of listening has on your relationships and what it's costing you and the others around you.

*Step 3: Shift your attention
from yourself and your survival
to others and the contribution
you can make to them*

Chapter 5

A New Way of Listening

Given how critical our listening is to our success in every aspect of our lives, it is amazing to me that we don't all have a profound understanding of the phenomenon of listening. This most basic of all human skills is simple to learn, yet I know of no school in the world that teaches it.

Listening consists of only two components. The first component is: Who do you have your attention on? The second component is: What's your internal conversation? That's it. All that "stuff" about body language, facial expression, eye contact, and the like flows directly from those two components. Understand them and you will unshackle yourself and acquire the freedom to be effective not only as a leader but in all your relationships.

Once you become aware of *how* you listen, which means becoming conscious of where you have your attention and your internal dialog when others are speaking to you, you can choose *not* to listen that way any longer. Implementing this choice will take focus, commitment and staying conscious. However, with practice you can train yourself to generate a different way of listening. Why would you want to do that?

To avoid the severe consequences associated with the ways of listening discussed in the previous chapter.

The first step is obvious. Since you have your attention on yourself when you listen unconsciously, you need to put your attention on the other person to generate a more constructive way of listening. That part is simple but critical in importance. While it's simple, it is not easy. Why? Because of that ego again. Remember, it's only concerned with its survival and tells you that everyone "out there" is the enemy. It does tell you that, which is why it's totally natural, in the world of your ego, to go through life with your attention on yourself.

Again, it's A or B. Listen to the ego or listen to your higher consciousness. Keep your attention on yourself or get it on the other person. The best part of training yourself in all of your interactions to get your total attention on the other person is that you don't hear the voice of the ego. It's a very effective way to take a break from the ego. Just focus your total attention on whoever you're with at the moment.

The tougher question is: What do you listen *for*?

Here are a few ways of listening to get the discussion started. You're sure to think of others as we go.

The Empowering Listening Filters

☙ *Listen for Possibility*

Would you like to learn how to totally suppress the creativity of the people around you? When they come to you with an idea that excites them, listen "get to the point," "find the flaw," "what am I going to say next," or "right/wrong."

Of course that's not what you want to do (even though in the past you may have unconsciously done exactly that).

Let's rephrase the question. Would you like to learn how to encourage people's creativity? Listen for *possibility*. Suppose someone is sharing one of his ideas with you. Instead of thinking about whether you like the idea or whether you think it would work or whether you agree with it, put your attention on him and ask yourself, "What's possible in this idea?" Manage your internal conversation to be inquisitive, to speculate with him, to be influenced by what he is saying. See if you can match his enthusiasm. Ask questions. Get into his reality. Work hard to see what he sees. You don't have to like it or agree with it. Just see the possibility.

This is a desirable way of listening for an executive because it *encourages* creativity in the workplace. Most leaders want their staff to be creative. However, when a staff member comes up with an idea the leader's default reaction is that they don't have time to listen, or that "they've done that before," or it won't work, or any of the other automatic ways of listening. That leader shouldn't be surprised if that's the last idea he hears from that staff member.

However, if you receive the idea with honest enthusiasm and see it through as far as you can, he will be encouraged to create another proposal even if you don't implement the initial idea. This is the power of *listening for possibility.*

❧ Listen for People's Commitment

Think of the last time someone came to you with a complaint. If you're like most leaders, you had your attention on yourself and were concerned with your survival. As you communicated with the complainer, your internal dialog probably went something like this: "Please, leave me alone. Can't you see I'm busy?" or "Here he comes again. How can I get rid of him this time so I can get back to what I have to do?"

I recently asked a group of speech attendees to share some of their reactions when they see a complaint coming. The answers were amusing. They would close their door, get on the phone, leave, hide, and go to the restroom.

Consider the possibility that in most cases, people complain to their boss because something isn't working and it's important to them that it works.

When people complain, they are saying that the thing that isn't working is keeping them from accomplishing something they are committed to. This is not always obvious when you don't listen for the other person's commitment.

This is the next desirable way of listening — *listening for people's commitment*. Get your attention off yourself, get it on the speaker, and manage your conversation to listen for what he or she is committed to.

I helped facilitate the resolution of a situation in an office between two secretaries that illustrates this way of listening. One secretary, Shirley, kept finding Sally's papers in, around, and on top of the copy machine every time she wanted to make a copy. It bothered her so she complained to the office manager, Lois. Since this had happened before, Lois was tired of her complaining and asked me what to do.

I told her that the next time Shirley complained, she should listen for her commitment and tell Shirley what she heard. Here's how it played out. Shirley walked into Lois's office, very upset, and said, "This is getting out of hand. Sally's papers are all over the copy machine and I can't get anything done."

Lois replied, "Let me understand this. What I hear is that you're committed to getting your work done in a timely and efficient manner and when Sally leaves her papers around the copy machine, that gets in the way of your commitment."

Shirley looked surprised (as will happen every time people have the experience of being heard). Lois reported that Shirley's upset disappeared. Rather than continue complaining, Shirley looked at Lois and said, "Yes, that's exactly right."

If you listen for someone's commitment and tell her what you hear, only two outcomes are possible. Either you'll get it right or you won't. Either way you win. If you get it right, she will respond as Shirley did. If you don't, she'll likely say something like, "No, that's not what I'm committed to. What I'm committed to is …"

Returning to Shirley and Lois, Lois then said, "Good, I thought so. I acknowledge you for your commitment to be a great secretary. Let's talk to Sally and find out what's going on with her and what she's committed to that prompts her to leave her papers at the copy machine."

By handling the situation the way she did, Lois took the circumstances out of the realm of right/wrong and good/bad, which is where most differences play out and why it's normally so difficult to reach resolution. Second, the phrase "all over the copy machine" is a judgment, not the truth. In confronting Sally, Lois needed to take that judgment out of the equation or Sally would feel she was being made wrong. There is no peace in a context of right/wrong. More about that later.

So Shirley and Lois paid Sally a visit. As coached, Lois said to Sally, "Shirley has been finding it difficult to get her work done as efficiently as she would like because of the delays she experiences when she has to make copies. Apparently, when she gets to the copy machine, she frequently finds your papers in the feeder or still in the sorter, and she has to remove them and find you before she can make her copies. (Notice, she stuck to the facts rather than being accusatory and using words like "you leave your papers all over the copy machine.") We're wondering what you're committed to that makes this happen." (Notice further that rather than being made wrong, Sally is actually being acknowledged. That makes it easy for her to tell the truth.)

Sally's answer was predictable. She wasn't a slob, careless or inconsiderate, all of which are judgments Shirley could have easily made. Rather, she said, "I'm working for four people. They have me running like crazy. And frankly, I'm overwhelmed. I'm in the middle of a job for one person and one of the others comes and grabs me to do something for her. Or I'm in the middle of a job and I go back to my desk to get something I need and one of them corners me. I'm really, really sorry. I can imagine what an upset this must be for you Shirley, but I don't mean to do it, and I just don't know what to do."

At this point, many possible solutions exist and it doesn't matter which one is chosen. What's important is that Shirley and Lois now have some understanding and compassion for Sally's situation. I guarantee you they'll work it out. In fact, what actually happened was that Shirley apologized to Sally for being so insensitive and volunteered to help her get her work done. They became great friends and teammates instead of adversaries. It happened because Lois listened for Shirley's commitment rather than shut her down, which we all too frequently do when someone complains.

❧ *Listening For the Gold*

Since your focus and your conversation determine the way you listen, another possible way to listen is *listening for the gold*. Zig Ziglar once told a story that demonstrates this way of listening.

As he told it, over a hundred years ago, Andrew Carnegie, the first great American industrialist, had many millionaires working for him. A newspaper reporter came to Mr. Carnegie and asked him how he was able to attract all of these millionaires to join his organization. His response, which surprised the reporter, was that none of them were millionaires when they came to work for him.

The reporter, now very curious, asked Mr. Carnegie how he developed these people to make them so valuable that he could afford to pay them enough that they became millionaires. Carnegie's answer: "Developing people is like mining for gold. When you go into a gold mine, you expect to take out a ton of dirt for every ounce of gold. But you go into the mine looking for the gold, not the dirt."

What he's suggesting is that inside of everyone is solid gold. Now I know it doesn't often look that way. We've all experienced the "jerks" of the world, which again is an interpretation and a judgment. Maybe there's a fabulous, wonderful person who, for some reason, is behaving badly. *Listening for the gold*, listening for the goodness in people, is a powerful way of listening and a way designed to allow the gold to show up. More about this later.

❧ Listen With Compassion

Are you are one of the rare people who never gets upset? Not likely. Trying to live your life without getting upset can be very upsetting. Human beings get upset; that's a fact. What's not so obvious is that upsets are almost always irrational. We develop an upset mechanism when we're very young and this mechanism stays with us for the rest of our lives. Whenever an event or person triggers the mechanism, we get upset. We know what triggered the mechanism so we *think* that is the cause of the upset (it's usually the person that pushed our button), but that's not the case. The upset is an illogical, built-in reaction to some event or circumstance.

I recently asked a group of speech attendees what they say when people around them get upset. I loved the answers: "chill out," "what are you getting so upset about?" "it will be OK," "relax," "take a Valium," "get over it," and "give it a break!"

As a leader, you don't ever want to say those things. When people are upset, they need a safe place to communicate their feelings. If you're willing to provide that, the upset will go away. How do you do that? *Listen with compassion.*

I first heard this discussed in 1989 when I was invited to join the Lew Epstein International Men's Club. Lew and his wife Francine had men's and women's clubs all around the country and one in London. Each month they would travel from city to city, meeting with groups of men and women.

The objective of the clubs was to provide a safe place for men and women to deal with the issues they faced in their relationships. In one of my earliest meetings, I remember Lew talking about us listening to each other with compassion, which he said was listening with a deep appreciation for *the other person's* feelings and experience. It's not listening to see how *you* feel or think about what the other person is saying, but how the other person feels about what he or she is saying.

In the years I was in the Club, I learned that in a conversation with another person, especially when they are upset, I could turn off my internal conversation and stop my constant judging of what the other person was saying. I could "get over there" with him, focus on what's going on with him, and re-create what he was feeling and experiencing.

Lew was a master at this. In the thirteen years I knew Lew, I never experienced him judging me or anyone else. When you were with Lew, he was with you, there for you, listening with all the empathy and compassion you can imagine. He was a true gift to us men and women, since we always knew that we were "safe" in his presence. He would not judge us, he wouldn't make us wrong, and he wouldn't even have an opinion about what we were doing or whom we were being. The result was that we could talk to him about anything and we were always confident that he wouldn't use it against us. What an incredible gift he was to all of us!

But what Lew did for us is not the point. The point is that you can do this too. You can be there for your staff, your employees, your customers, your spouse, your children and your friends as Lew was for us. You can make it safe for the people in your life to talk to you and tell you what's on their minds. You can provide a safe space for them to resolve their upsets. You can have them feel like you're there for them and give them the experience of being heard. Listen for the gold and listen with compassion. That's it. Nothing else is required. As Lew would say, "It's simple, not easy." It is simple, but it takes daily practice and a huge commitment on your part to master so you can reap the rewards that come with this way of listening.

One last thing. When you're upset, be very careful about what comes out of your mouth. Remember, your upset is irrational. You think you know why you're upset, but you really don't. Don't attack; don't lash out. Lew used to tell us to say: "I'm upset, I'm really upset." Keep it simple. Find a person who will listen to your upset with compassion so you can let it go.

๖ Win/Win

Another very powerful way to listen in business is *win/win*. Instead of listening to see if you are going to win, without paying attention to whether the other person wins as well (which, quite frankly, is what you find in most businesses), put your attention on the other person and find ways for him to win in the transaction, too.

For many years I coached Joe, a company president, as he steadily grew his business. Working with Joe was a great joy because he took this way of listening, which he called *win/win/win,* to the highest level. As they developed new products, new packaging, and new advertising, he would ask, "How is the company going to win, how are all our employees and stakeholders going to win, and how is the customer going to win?" People in the company learned quickly that they had better figure it all out before presenting a proposal to Joe. His commitment was that everyone wins.

I'm not asserting that Joe's way is the "right" way to listen while running a company. However, it seemed then and seems now to be a "smart" way. It's been my experience that you can only play the win/lose game for so long. Sooner or later, people will catch on to your game. And that doesn't even address the fact that you have to be able to sleep at night. History has proven that companies that operate from the perspective of everybody winning, including the environment, the community, and the nation, come out ahead in the long run.

Ꮼ *And/Both*

The final way of listening I want to suggest is what I call *and/both*. In the unconscious ways of listening we had *either/or*, as in "You can't have your cake and eat it too" or "It's either going to be this way or that way." With *either/or*, somebody wins and somebody loses. Somebody has to compromise.

Who says? Maybe it doesn't have to be that way. After all, it's just a conversation in the existing paradigm. Like all of the other conversations, we're not stuck with it. Instead, listen to determine ways where you don't have to choose, where nobody has to compromise, where you can both/all have it your way, and where you get to have your cake and eat it too. Will you always be able to figure out a way "to have it all?" Sometimes yes and sometimes no. But why not try? You have everything to gain and nothing to lose.

The Conscious Listening Advantage

You could certainly generate other ways of listening, but listening for possibility, listening for commitment, listening for the gold, listening with compassion, listening win/win, and listening and/both are my favorites. In all of these ways, you keep your attention on the other person as you manage your conversation.

What are the advantages of listening in one or more of these ways? Recall the list of consequences you experience when you listen with your attention on yourself and in one of the unconscious ways. The opposite of all those consequences now becomes what's available to you with these new ways of listening.

You get real communication, understanding, intimacy, trust and an appreciation of the other person's position. That creates satisfaction, happiness, a sense of well being, self-confidence, joy, aliveness and ultimately rich, meaningful, quality relationships. In a business setting, the payoff is productivity, creativity, teamwork, enthusiasm, no turnover, success and of course money, results and accomplishment. You get all of this by switching the way you listen.

What do you have to give up to get these benefits? Only the need to be right, to win, to have it your way, and to focus on yourself to the exclusion of others. These aren't things humans find it easy to give up. However, it's a worthy trade. I invite you to take it.

Again, life, while not easy, is simple. A or B. Go through life with your attention on yourself, which is what the ego wants you to do, or go through life with your attention on others, which is what *you* really want to do. Choose. There's a lot riding on that choice.

Summary and Unshackled Leadership Action Items

Listening consists of only two components. The first component is: Who do you have your attention on? The second component is: What's your internal conversation? That's it.

1. In every interaction during the next week, make a conscious effort to stop whatever you're doing, give your undivided attention to the other person and listen for the gold.
2. In brainstorming sessions, listen for possibility.
3. If someone comes to you with a complaint, listen for what they are committed to.
4. To the degree that you are successful in giving your undivided attention to another person when in a conversation with them, begin to notice the impact that way of being has on the relationship:

   a. Do you experience a greater level of intimacy?
   b. Do you experience a greater level of trust?
   c. Do you leave the interaction feeling better about yourself and them?
   d. Do you have an overall sense of well-being and a new sense of peacefulness?

The problem in my life and other people's lives is not the absence of knowing what to do but the absence of doing it.
• Peter Drucker

The important thing is this: to be able at any moment to sacrifice what we are for what we could become.
• Charles DuBois

Chapter 6

The Nature of Our Reality

This might seem overly simple and too good to be true, but can you think of anything you do at work that doesn't involve either speaking or listening or both? Even when you're alone in your office? Everything we do lives in a conversation. In fact, our ability to have a conversation is what distinguishes human beings from other species in the animal kingdom.

What's missing for people in general and leaders in particular is an appreciation of the phenomenon of listening and the power of speaking. The good news is that in the last two chapters, you have come to know everything you need to know to become an effective listener. Now it's time to turn our attention to the other side of the coin. Let's look at the nature of our reality and how we use language in the existing paradigm.

We wake up in the morning, look out into our world and observe what we observe. We take in whatever we see occurring at the time and, as the observer, we create an explanation for what we see. I use the word "world" to encompass everything we see, including our company, our spouse, our children, our employees, the competition, the economy and everything else.

Have you ever asked yourself the question, "How come I see what I see?" Interesting question. If you listen carefully to how people speak, you will find that people think they see what they see because they are sure it "is" the way they see it.

In other words, while it is not the case with all people all of the time, most of us believe that our explanation is "the truth" — that "it" and "them" are the way we see "it" and "them." Think about that. Don't you think that you see your children, your parents, your spouse, your employees, your job, your business, the economy, and the competition the way you see them because that's how they actually are? "That's just the way (fill in the blank) is," we say.

You may never have thought about this before and that's okay. Remember, the purpose of our time together is to get you to look at what is right in front of you, that you may take for granted and may have never thought about, and see it in a new way. That's why I'm asking you to think about this now.

You are an intelligent person. You have eyes. You can see and process information. That's why you think what you see is real. To you, it's the truth. If you think about it, you will see that's exactly what happens.

You think there is a reality and you see it. Then you open your mouth to speak about what you see. You describe or "talk about" it. If you doubt you do this, spend a day listening to other people speak. If you listen to others without judging them, you will discover that in most instances, people use language to "talk about" or describe the world they think they see. They think they are speaking the truth!

Pick a day and record everything you say on a voice recorder. That night listen to the recording. You will find that you spent the vast majority of your day talking about the way you think "it" is.

For example, in hundreds of discussions with company executives I've asked them to tell me about their company, their employees, the economy, the competition, and so on. In every case, they answer my questions as if they are relating "facts." Rarely do they realize they do this.

Many years ago, in a conversation with an old friend, I shared how much I enjoy people, how fun I find them to be, how gracious I think most people are and how much I enjoy meeting new people (more about this later). He quickly replied, "Yes, but that's just on the surface. If you go below, you will find that all people are up to no good, they are devious, self seeking and mostly dishonest. You really ought to watch yourself with people."

"Really?" I replied. "What has you say that?"

"That's just the truth about people. If you paid attention, you'd see that's the way they are."

I could see that there was no point arguing with him. He "knew" how people "are." I don't know what happened that caused him to reach that conclusion, but that's the conclusion he reached. There was no other possibility. It wasn't *his* truth; it was *the* truth.

As the conversation continued, he shared more of his "truths." *All* politicians are crooked, the plan to rebuild the world trade center was ridiculous, exercise isn't fun, his children don't care about him, it takes "forever" to get medical devices approved by the government, and on and on and on. He stated everything not as an observation or an opinion, but as a fact.

Think about it. If there were a reality or "truth" and we all had the ability to accurately see and describe what was there, then wouldn't everyone see and describe the same thing? Your immediate answer is probably "no" because you know that everyone doesn't see the same thing. But reread the question I asked. The answer, as I posed the question, is "of course." If there was a reality or "truth" and we all could see it, then we should, by definition, all see the same thing.

The reality is that we all *don't* see the same thing. Everyone sees something different. Everyone has his or her own perception. We all have times when we are absolutely sure something or somebody is a particular way. We need to get others to see "it" or "them" that way but they just don't. They are convinced that it's another way because they are different observers.

If you think about this logically, then what I'm saying will be evident. We all see what we see for reasons we will explore in a moment. That's the way it is. Everyone lives in a different reality. Everyone sees the world through a unique set of eyes. Therefore, does it make sense to use language to describe or "talk about" what's there? After all, who knows what's really there? There's only what you observe. So if you use language *only* to describe what *you* observe, with no attachment to whether it's the truth, then there's no harm done. However, that rarely occurs.

Truth or Perception?

So what's really going on? What is the nature of our reality? What is the true function of language? Consider this possibility: We wake up in the morning, look out into our world, and see what we see, just as we've discussed before. There's still some phenomenon going on and you're still the observer.

But what makes you the observer you are? What do you wake up into? The answer is the "conversation" — the one that you've been developing since day one. Here are two ways to look at what actually happens. Specifically, you either:

- Project your conversation onto the world you see and see your individualized version of whatever is there; or
- You interpret what you observe through a filtering mechanism that your conversation controls.

Here's another way of looking at this. We think we see with our eyes. That's not the truth, as amazing as it is for me to assert that. We actually see with our mind. Rather than being receivers, our eyes are like projectors, projecting whatever is going on in our minds onto the blank screen of life. It's like going to the movies. During the movie, all the action seems to take place on the screen. Actually what's in front of you is a blank screen. The movie only exists on the film in the projector. The projector lens projects the movie onto the screen.

Are you with me? Here's an example: You have an employee. Your conversation is that he's lazy. Is that "the truth?" Who knows? You certainly have evidence that he's lazy, but that "evidence" could justify any one of a number of other conclusions. Perhaps his wife isn't well and he's preoccupied with her health. Maybe his kids are having problems in school. Perhaps he's going through a divorce. Who knows? All you know is that he acts in a certain way and you've interpreted his behavior as being lazy.

As a result, you walk into work in the morning and there's that lazy guy. You talk with others about what to do with this lazy employee. Even if he works hard one day, you think he's up to something, because, after all, he's lazy. In your world, he is that way.

Here's another example: In the early '80s, interest rates rose to 20+%. Lots of people fled from the residential real estate business because they assumed that with interest rates that high, nobody would buy houses, making sales impossible. Their interpretation of the events of the day told them to quit the business because they could do nothing to change the situation.

Yet I know a man who came to this country from India at the height of the inflation scare. He decided to sell real estate. Over the next few years, while many quit the business, he became rich. Why? He didn't realize that interest rates weren't always that high and, with his strong commitment to creating success, he saw opportunities, not impossibilities.

Now let's consider this truth. There is no world "out there" that *is* a particular way. There is no "reality." Yes, some physical, objective realities exist, such as the person who works for you, interest rates, and the economy, but we don't relate to those *things*. We only relate to our *interpretation* and our *explanation* of what we see.

Is what we see "the truth" or our interpretation? I say it's *always* our interpretation — that is, *you* are the source of what you see. You interpret everything based on how you learned to interpret things when you were young, filtering everything through your conversation. That's why everyone has different opinions and perceptions. There isn't something different out there for everyone to see; rather, everyone is a different observer who interprets things differently.

The True Function of Language

This brings us back to language and its function. If language's purpose is not to talk about or describe what's there, then what *is* its function?

When I ask this question in a workshop or a speech, the answers I receive are usually quite funny, at least to me. The most common answer is "to convince others that what we see is really the truth." We certainly do that. Another is "to share our reality." Sometimes we do that as well. Some people say, "to express our opinion (which we rarely 'own' as just our opinion; we usually speak our opinion as 'the truth')." Another common answer is "to ask questions so we can find out what other people see." All of these responses are valid uses of language.

Consider, though, that the fundamental purpose of language is to create and invent with. Language is primarily a tool of creation. You are the source of what you see — it's all your interpretation — and every time you open your mouth, you are *not describing* what's there; rather, you are speaking into existence what's there, *for you.* No, it's not *the truth*; it's only *your truth!* **We don't describe the world we see — we see the world we describe!**

You Create Your Reality Every Time You Open Your Mouth

Imagine you and I are walking in the woods. We come around the bend in the trail and see standing in front of us a big black bear. What's your conversation? Most people answer: "Oh my God! What am I going to do? This is scary! Should I run, play dead, yell for help?" Because that is their conversation, they react with fear.

I remember the first time this actually happened to me. In 1980 a friend and I backpacked into Yosemite National Park. We had hiked up the trail from Tenaya Lake on our way to Sunrise High Sierra Camp, where we planned to spend the night.

For some reason my friend and I got separated and I was walking alone along the trail. I came around a bend and there in front of me, no more than ten yards away, was a big black bear. I stopped. The excitement of the moment hit me. To be that close to a bear in the wilderness was thrilling. I was not the slightest bit scared. I had thought about the possibility of this moment in advance and *my* conversation was that, for the most part, bears are friendly. They want your food, not you. As long as you don't act stupid you have nothing to worry about.

What's "the truth?" Should you be afraid or excited? Are bears scary and dangerous or are they playful, cute and safe? I don't know. And I don't care. I only know what's true for me. And what's true for me is whatever I say!

The same goes for you. What's true for you, *in every area of your life and your business,* is whatever *you* say. This is important to understand because our actions are always a response to the world we see. Unfortunately, we don't realize that *we* make up the world we see, and that we do it with language.

(By the way, the bear didn't attack me or threaten me. It looked at me for a moment and then went on with its business, walking back into the woods, leaving me wanting more.)

Life is Like a Tennis Game

An analogy might be helpful at this point. Think of a tennis match. In any game of tennis, a very different game is going on in the stands than the game being played on the court. In the stands, the people watching the game have a conversation that goes something like this: "Boy, does he have a great forehand! His backhand is a bit weak, but his serve is really good. And look how quickly he gets to the net. Wow! What an overhead."

In the stands, there are forehands and backhands and serves and overheads. But that's not what's happening on the court. There the player is following the ball and trying his or her best to hit it over the net. If he is standing on one side of the court and the opponent hits the ball to the other side, he runs over there and hits the ball. If the opponent hits a drop shot, he runs forward and hits the ball. And so it goes.

Everyone who has ever played tennis knows that on the court, there are no forehands, no backhands and no overheads. There's just a player following the ball and trying to hit it. The player's actions are always in response to how the ball shows up *to the player* as it comes across the net.

Many years ago Stefan Edberg played Boris Becker in the finals at Wimbledon. Stefan Edberg won the match. As I watched him play, I remember thinking that he must be in "the zone"

I've heard athletes talk about because he played so well. As he left the court after his win, Bud Collins interviewed him. He asked Stefan what it was like for him during the match and why he thought he played so well.

Stefan's response is something I'll never forget. He said, "As the match wore on, the ball got bigger and bigger and it came across the net slower and slower. I got to the point where I knew I would make every shot."

What was Stefan doing? He was responding to how the ball showed up and that's what happens on the court in any tennis match.

As a former tennis player, I think about what it would be like for me to stand on a tennis court with Andy Roddick serving the ball at 140+ miles per hour. The ball would likely look like a pea shot out of a cannon. However, today's great tennis players see the ball differently, more like what Stefan Edberg saw in his match with Boris Becker. They often have little difficulty returning Andy's serve.

The same thing happens in the game of life. Our actions are always in response to how the world in front of us shows up for us (and, again, I use the word "world" to refer to whatever is in front of us at the moment). So our actions in business are in response to how our employees, our competitors, or the economy show up for us. I hope this is evident.

What may not be evident is that we mostly think it's "them" or "it" (our competitors or our employees, for example) that makes them or it show up for us the way they do. So we think the economy "is" a particular way, and that's why it occurs for us the way it does. The same happens with our business, the competition, and our employees. As stated before, we use language to describe or talk about the way our business, the competition, and the economy, is.

This mentality is like continuing to live as if the earth were flat when we now know that it's round. What's worse is that this thinking turns you into a victim. You believe that events are outside the realm of your control and that your only choice is to react or respond to circumstances that someone or something else created.

To the contrary, I suggest that *you* determine the way your world shows up for you. As I said earlier, your eyes project the conversation that you have about whatever or whoever is in front of you onto what's there. When you open your mouth and talk about the economy, your business, or the competition, you are actually speaking that reality into existence. Then you act on it as if it were the truth. However, it's only the truth for you and only because you thought and said it!

This is the second and most important attribute of the new paradigm leader we're creating. Being a powerful, effective and "conscious" leader means:

- You realize that what you see is your perception
- You understand that you create your perception all the time; you do it whenever you open your mouth to speak
- You are responsible for what you say
- You accept the consequences of what you think and speak.

Other attributes are the flip side of the above points:

- You realize that what other people say is merely their perception;
- You understand that what comes out of their mouth is only their truth, whether they realize it or not;
- You hold them responsible for what they say; and
- You allow them to accept the consequences for what they think and speak.

Creating Your Reality

Your tongue is like a paintbrush. Every time you open your mouth, you paint a picture of a world. Then you *and everyone around you* live in that world as if it were the truth. But it's not *the* truth; it's only *your* truth. The question is, are you doing this responsibly and thinking deeply about what you say and how you say it, or are you doing it unconsciously and irresponsibly? Once again, A or B.

Consider that over six billion people live on the planet and that they have over six billion different realities. Everyone's "reality" is a figment of his or her imagination. So few people actually see this. Consider my friend who exemplifies this point. He actually thought that what he was saying about people is "the truth." If I even suggested that maybe it wasn't *the* truth, just *his* truth, he'd be insulted and get defensive. He's not unique. Look at the extent to which you do the same thing!

When you think your explanation of what's going on in front of you is the "truth," that's the end of the discussion. If you're committed to your point of view, you're stuck. But if you realize that it's *all* your interpretation, that it's *all* up for discussion, then you have enormous power.

Why? Because *how* we explain and interpret the world we live in leads to very different courses of action. Suppose your daughter comes home from school with a bad report card. Lots of explanations are available: she's not smart, she's lazy, her friends are a bad influence, or she has a lousy teacher. The explanation you give yourself determines the course of action you take.

If you think she's not very smart, you get her a tutor. If you think she's lazy, you do what you can to motivate her. If you think her friends are a bad influence, you try to convince her to find new friends. If you think she has a lousy teacher, you talk to the teacher or the principal. This is why it's crucial to understand that these are all interpretations and that being a conscious observer is the key.

Summary and Unshackled Leadership Action Items

Because we are intelligent human beings, we have no reason to think that whatever we see might not be the truth. That's almost illogical. However, the reality is that what we "see" with our eyes is always a projection of whatever thoughts we are having about whatever or whoever is in front of us in the moment. Therefore the function of language is *not* to describe what's "there" but to create our reality. Every time you open your mouth, you literally speak your reality into existence.

1. The first step in transforming your consciousness is to begin to see what's there. Start this week by thinking about the above summary statement and inquiring into its validity. Map it onto your experience.

2. Ask yourself why you see things the way you do. Are people the way you see them or are you seeing them based on some judgment you have about them, maybe formed long ago.

3. Start noticing how other people speak. Are they being responsible for their statements and speaking *their* truth as *their* truth or are they speaking *their* truth as *the* truth.

4. What about you?

5. Are you committed to your interpretations or are you open to the possibility that it's all interpretation?

*Step 5: Get that happiness,
satisfaction and fulfillment
are choices you make*

Chapter 7

The Nature of Satisfaction and Happiness

There is an almost endless list of examples of why it's critical, if you are going to become an unshackled leader, to understand that you use language for creation rather than description. For instance, let's explore the nature of satisfaction.

Most people determine whether they are satisfied or not by how they view the circumstances they experience. We look at our circumstances, judge whether the circumstances are the way we would like them to be, and if they are we're satisfied and if they're not we're dissatisfied.

When you live this way, your circumstances determine your satisfaction. You're like a weather vane in a storm, with your level of satisfaction changing at the whim of your life circumstances.

Consider that in any given situation, your inner conversation can be anything. You can be desperately poor and profoundly satisfied or fabulously wealthy and completely miserable. It's all a matter of what you think and how you *choose to interpret* your circumstances.

So what if you decide to start from a state of satisfaction? What if you decide that your life is whatever it is, that you're satisfied, and then go forth from there? Think how wonderful it would be to stop trying so hard to get to satisfaction. Imagine how much more powerful it would be to start from a state of satisfaction and then take your satisfaction with you wherever you go.

A Fundamental Reality of Life

Now, here's the real rub. You can't get to any place other than where you start from.

If you "say" you're dissatisfied, for whatever reason, perhaps because you don't like your circumstances, and then set out to get to satisfaction, what do you take with you every step of the way? Dissatisfaction! With such baggage, you'll never know when you arrive at your destination. Your experience will be like a hamster on a tread wheel. No matter how good the circumstances get, you're always seeking more and better because you're standing in a place of dissatisfaction.

At times things seem to click and you say "this is it." How long does that last? Not very long. You soon find yourself back in a place of dissatisfaction. It's a lot easier and a lot more fun to decide, right now, that you're satisfied and take that mindset with you on your journey into the future.

How do you develop such a mindset? Here's a start: Consider that if you had the money to buy this book, you're one of the luckier people alive. Over 20,000 people die every day from starvation. Millions of people around the world live in poverty. Half the people on the planet have never used a telephone and a lot more don't have computers or cell phones or fax machines — all those wonderful modern conveniences we take for granted. When you look at the condition of life on our planet, it makes sense to be profoundly grateful for how wonderful our lives truly are.

By the way, this is not about "positive thinking." Every day people die, planes crash, accidents happen, crimes occur, and people do bad things to each other. I'm not ignoring the realities of life. Fortunately, there's plenty of room in the context of satisfaction for the entire range of human emotions. Will you be satisfied all the time? Of course not. But when you're committed to being satisfied, you take your licks and rebound a lot faster; you get over the sadness or the hurt or the anger, and you get back to doing your work. Rather than being about positive thinking, this discussion is about taking responsibility for your life and not being a victim.

One day several months ago, the day started with the news that a prospective client had decided to proceed with the project we had discussed. I was elated. A short time later, a speech I expected to get was given to someone else. I had worked hard to get the engagement and was frustrated and disappointed. Later in the day, a friend made a remark that sounded insulting and made me angry. And to top it all off, an e-mail came telling me that my cousin, who had been battling a life threatening disease for quite a while, had died.

As you can imagine, there are many ways to interpret such a day. In the past, I might have said, "Oh well, you win some and you lose some." The parts I liked would be "good" and the parts I didn't like would be "bad." I remember this day clearly because that's *not* how I looked at it. Given my commitment to be satisfied, I remember saying to myself, "What an amazing day. What a gift it is to be alive. In the course of one day I experienced the entire range of human emotions. One minute I was thrilled, the next disappointed, the next angry, the next sad, and then back to being thrilled. Wow! How extraordinary. How blessed I am to have such freedom." Strange? No. Different? Surely.

When you put these ideas into practice you set a wonderful example, which is one of the keys to empowering leadership. Remember, your tongue is like a paintbrush. Every time you open your mouth, you paint a picture of a world and then you *and everyone around you* lives into that world as if it were the truth. So if you're satisfied and grateful, then words of satisfaction and gratitude come out of your mouth, which is highly motivating to the people around you. Satisfaction and gratitude are contagious.

Unfortunately, dissatisfaction and complaining are also contagious. So if words of dissatisfaction and complaints come out of your mouth, then you will be de-motivating the people around you. Which mindset do you choose? A or B?

Happiness

Another example that demonstrates that language is a vehicle of creation is the nature of happiness. How do you normally determine whether you are happy? In Western culture, many people think they will be happy when they achieve the "American Dream." You know — the house with the white picket fence, the Mercedes, the weekend cottage at the lake. Madison Avenue knows how desperately we want this dream life, which is why all advertising attempts to convince us that we will be a lot happier if we use the product or service they promote. You might just do exactly this in your company's advertising.

I suggest that happiness, like satisfaction, has little to do with our circumstances. You're either willing to be happy or you're not. It's a choice you make. Just like satisfaction, happiness lives in your conversation. In her book *Real Moments* (Dell Publishing, 1994), Barbara DeAngelis, Ph.D. says, "Happiness is a choice you make in each moment about how you experience that moment, not a state you one day achieve." So you either choose to be happy or you don't. And your choice is reflected in what you say. Once again, A or B!

One day while I was giving a speech, some words slipped out of my mouth that I had never spoken before. I'm not sure where the thought came from, but I have since repeated it numerous times. Here it is: at any given moment, 99.9999+% of the things in our lives are working absolutely perfectly. The earth rotates around its axis every day, staying exactly the right distance from the sun so we don't get too hot or too cold. Fresh air is all around for us to breathe. Our heart and other organs do their thing. All these events happen without any input from us.

From that perspective, it must follow that only .oo...01% of the things in our lives are not working absolutely perfectly. With that in mind, where do we focus our attention? Instead of waking up in the morning and saying, "Another day in paradise," noticing the 99.9999+% of the things that are working perfectly, without any input from us, and being grateful for the sheer privilege it is to be alive, we focus on and complain about the .oo...01% of the things that are not the way we want them to be. Unbelievable? Yes. But it's true. Sometimes I think we are truly insane.

Recently, at a speech I gave at a convention in Las Vegas, I asked the attendees, "How many of you wake up in the morning into a conversation which is some version of 'another day in paradise'?" No hands went up. When you stop to think about it, isn't that sad?

At any moment, regardless of the circumstances, you can choose to be happy and satisfied, to appreciate and feel grateful for what you already have, and to stop waiting for life to turn out better. Because you know what? Your life has already turned out. This is what it looks like when it turns out. This. Right now. It all lives in your thinking and your conversation.

So this is it. Choose. Are you satisfied or not? Are you happy or not? A or B? Are you listening to the voice of your ego, which will always have you be dissatisfied and unhappy, or are you listening to your higher consciousness?

Actually, the ego is amazingly effective at generating disempowering conversations. One of the favorite conversations of the ego is what we call "when — then!" It has you believe that you will be happy/satisfied when... fill in the blank. The ego will *always* have you believe that your source of satisfaction and happiness lies outside of yourself.

Another favorite conversation of the ego is what we call "if only." You would surely be happy and satisfied if only... fill in the blank. The ego loves to have you feel like a victim. If Joe would only... If my employees would only... If I could only come up with the right marketing message. Make your own list of what if only's it's been feeding you.

Still another ego game is to present to you unsolvable problems or to ask you unanswerable questions. When you find yourself dealing with a problem you can't find a solution to or asking yourself a question you can't find a satisfactory answer to, you know it's the work of the ego.

If you're saying to yourself at this moment: "I can't believe the ego is that vicious," guess again. It is. As I said earlier, your ego is not your friend. It is public enemy number one. If you want to be an effective leader, if you want to come from joy, satisfaction and happiness, you must learn to turn down or ignore the voice of the ego and turn up or focus on the voice of your higher consciousness.

As a leader, your choice impacts not only you, but everyone in your organization and the organization itself. It's an important choice, so choose wisely. A or B. Choose.

Summary and Unshackled Leadership Action Items

Dealing with our ego voice is the biggest challenge for a leader. It will always tell you that your satisfaction and happiness lie outside of you, that you get to be satisfied and happy by manipulating the circumstances and the people in your life to be the way you want them to be. To make matters worse, the ego sets up impossible challenges to make sure that you never accomplish your goal.

1. Ask yourself honestly: are you satisfied or not?
2. If the answer isn't a resounding "yes," can you see that it's only because the circumstances of your life and/or your business are not the way you would like them to be?
3. Are you open to the possibility that you can choose to be satisfied and take your satisfaction with you as you work on those same circumstances? After all, what's the

likelihood that your circumstances will *ever* be exactly as you would like?

4. Ask the same questions regarding your happiness. If you're not happy, can you see that you've bought into the belief that happiness comes from outside of us, from the people and circumstances in our lives?

5. Spend time this week practicing being happy just for the sake of being happy. Start seeing happiness as a choice you make, not something that happens to you.

*Step 6: Let go of your judgments
about people and look for the
gold in them instead*

Chapter 8

Our Relationship to People

In all of our relationships, the way we use language once again creates our reality. Here's how it works. Ordinarily we relate to people by judging and assessing them. We meet someone and within the first few seconds we judge or assess him or her. No wonder we don't get a second chance to make a good first impression.

In workshops and speeches I ask people to say some of the not-so-nice words they have heard come out of their mouths during this process of judging and assessing people. The list that evolves includes jerk, idiot, ugly, cheap, lazy, arrogant, self-centered, selfish, stupid, impatient, dishonest, incompetent, inconsiderate and much more. Some of the things people say are not fit to print. In any event, it's not a pretty list. Have you heard yourself use some or all of these words?

Then I ask, "What's possible in how we relate to people?" Given that language creates our reality, couldn't we invent who people are? What a novel concept. The question then becomes, "What are some of the empowering words we *could* say about people?" That list includes wonderful, smart, clever, honest, talented, creative, team player, contributor, caring, patient, generous, brilliant, loving, gorgeous and fabulous.

Here's the $64,000 question: "What's the 'truth' about people?" Some of the answers are "a little of both," "someplace in the middle," "depends," "sometimes one and sometimes the other."

What's your answer?

I say that there is no "truth" about people. Better yet, I don't know what the truth is about people. I'm not that smart. Do you know what "the truth" is? I only know what's true for me. I suggest that what's true for you is what's true only for you. Your truth is what *you* decide!

Golden Wisdom

My first insight into what I am suggesting came in the late 1980s. I had a coaching company and received a contract to work with and coach thirty real estate agents in an office that was not doing well. I did the project as a joint venture with Amba Gale, the owner of another coaching company. Together we produced dramatic results. In five months, the average agent increased productivity by approximately 300% and this office went from being the least profitable in the region to the most profitable in the state.

The regional VP was so thrilled with the results that he hired us to work with the other offices in the region. Amba didn't personally want to continue with the project so she sent one of her employees, Rita Reneaux, to work with me on future projects.

On the first day of the next project, Rita and I stood at the front of the room as the agents walked in for their first coaching session. As always, and without realizing I was doing so, I made my usual judgments and assessments of each person. Yet I couldn't help but notice how excited Rita was becoming as each person entered the room. I couldn't imagine what was going on with her.

At the end of the day, I asked Rita, "What was going on with you this morning when the people were coming into the room?"

She looked at me quizzically and replied, "What are you talking about?"

I said, "When the people were coming in, you got more and more excited by the minute and I couldn't understand why. They looked like a pretty ragged group to me; some even seemed unfriendly. I thought we were going to have quite a time working with this group, but you didn't seem to have the same thoughts at all."

Finally understanding my question, she smiled. "I saw one more wonderful person after another coming in the room and that's why I was so excited."

I looked at her in amazement and jokingly asked, "Are you on drugs or something? One more wonderful person after another? Are you kidding?"

Understanding my confusion, she said, "Scott, if you went looking for gold, would you find it lying on the ground, or would you have to dig in the dirt to find it?" This was my first experience with the "gold story" discussed earlier.

"Well," I replied, "you would likely have to dig in the dirt for it."

Then she said something that would ultimately change my life: "People are the same way. Inside of *every* human being is a bar of solid gold. But it's often covered up with all kinds of 'dirt' they picked up when they were two and three and four and fourteen years old. Now the question is, 'What will you go looking for?' Whatever it is, I promise you will always find it. If you stop looking when you see the dirt, so be it. But if you look deeply, you'll almost always find the gold!"

Consider that there is no "truth" about people. There's only what's true for you. If you give yourself permission to judge and assess people, you'll see only your own judgments and assessments. However, if you decide in advance that all people are brilliant, gorgeous, talented, and fabulous, and go looking for that, then you will see that far more often.

Some Important Back-Story Truisms

That day Rita got me thinking deeply about this subject. I have come, many years later, to understand four powerful back-story truisms that impact our relationships with all people. To me a "truism" is something that works not just some of the time, but *all* of the time. It's like gravity — if you drop something, it goes down, every single time. That's why it's a truism.

Back-Story Truism #1: You will always find what you go looking for.

If you think the world is full of jerks, you'll find lots of them. If you think people are wonderful, you'll find a lot of wonderful people.

Now you might say, "Yes, but you don't know _____ (insert any name here). He really *is* a jerk!"

I say he isn't. He's a brilliant, gorgeous, talented, fabulous person who, for some reason, because of some belief, *at times,* may act like a jerk. But do you see him all of the time? How do you know how he acts in different situations and with different people? Because you've labeled him a jerk, you won't see all the times when he doesn't act that way.

Someone reading the above recently asked me an interesting question. "So if you don't find what you go looking for does that mean you're looking in the wrong place?"

"No," I said, "you're missing the point. This is not about looking for a 'thing' and wondering why you can't find it. This is a truism in life. If you think people are great, you'll see lots of great people. If you think your business has lots of opportunities for success, you'll find opportunities. If you think that you have lots of problems, you'll find problems all over the place."

Many years ago, I worked with the partners of a large law firm headquartered in San Francisco. My project with them lasted for six months so I got to know all the partners well. When the job was complete, the firm's chairman took me aside and said, "You have to help me do something with John (not his real name). He's the manager of the Los Angeles office and he has everyone upset. He's a great lawyer, but he's angry all of the time, and I'm about to have a revolt down there."

I looked into the situation, talked to many of the associates in the Los Angeles office, and found that he had told me the truth. They all thought John was some version of "jerk." I don't remember their exact words, but none of them liked him. They thought he was awful to deal with, that he yelled all the time, and that he needed to go. They were at the point where if he didn't leave, they would.

I was stunned. I had worked with John for six months and found him to be a gracious, compassionate and generally friendly guy. Was I crazy? Why didn't I see his "jerk" factor? I decided to meet with John. It was a meeting I'll never forget. Here's how it went.

I started by saying, "John, I hear that you get angry a lot and yell at people. Is that the truth?"

He hesitated for a moment and then somewhat sheepishly replied, "Yes, I guess it is."

Sensing his willingness to be open, I asked, "Well, why do you do that?"

His answer was interesting. He said, "I have this group of smart, talented lawyers that work in this office. I don't see any of them putting in the effort necessary to live up to their potential. Sometimes it seems like they do just enough to get by and it really irritates me."

I could have gone down the tunnel of saying, "Boy, what a jerk!" But given my "conversation" that all people are wonderful and *almost always* have a good motive for what they do, and listening for his commitment, I heard something that I thought would get me to the bottom of his behavior.

My reply was, "So, you have these people around you who you don't see working very hard and you think that getting angry and yelling will motivate them to get into action and do the job you think they are capable of!"

He looked at me and said, "You know, I never thought about it that way. But now that I hear what you just said, I'd say you were exactly right." (By the way, these are the gems you hear when you look for the gold that you never hear when you judge and assess people and call them a jerk.)

I then said, "Interesting strategy. Does it work?"

"Heck no," he said. "And what's worse, they hate me."

So I said, "Why do you continue doing it?"

He replied, "I don't know what else to do!"

Do you get it? He had a legitimate objective, to motivate his staff to put in the effort necessary to fulfill their potential, but he had come up with an unworkable strategy to meet his objective. The more he tried to implement the strategy, the less it worked. The result was that the people around him saw him as a "jerk," not as a good guy with a bad strategy. Had they been trained to listen for the gold and listen for people's commitment, as I'm asking you to do, they could have had the same conversation with him that I did, and I wouldn't have had to get involved.

Such a scenario is typical with people. They develop ineffective strategies, probably at age four or five, to accomplish legitimate objectives, and continue to play out those strategies despite the negative outcomes. They then get more and more frustrated along the way, even though they know it's not working, *because they don't know what else to do!* Instead of us being compassionate and understanding, given the pain they must be in, we label them jerk, idiot, or arrogant and the game is over. (I'll talk more in Chapter 12 about what the payoff is for us when we do that and what it costs us.)

Getting back to John, I next said to him, "If I could show you a strategy that was designed to accomplish your legitimate objective, eliminate your need to get angry, and actually get people to like you, would you be interested?"

"Of course," he said.

On a piece of paper I drew two parallel lines representing the two sides of a river. Between them I drew a few squiggly lines representing the water.

"Let's make believe the lawyers in your office are standing on one side of this river and you want to get them to the other side," I said. "Let's say that the water is ice cold and running too fast for them to swim. Can you see that no amount of yelling will get them to jump in and swim to the other side?"

"Sure," he said.

I continued, "Suppose we put a bunch of big rocks in the river, close together, so it wouldn't be too difficult to get from one to the other, and put them all the way across. Now, what if you told them to step on only the first rock? What if you assured them that you had all the confidence in the world in their ability to do that, to not worry about the rest of the rocks, and to focus only on the first rock and give it a try? Do you think they would do that?"

Again, he said, "Sure."

"Okay. What if, when they got on the first rock, you congratulate them, tell them how much you knew they could do it, how proud you are of them, and how much you appreciate their courage and willingness to take that first step? Do you think they would feel good about themselves, or perhaps have a newfound confidence in themselves?"

"I would imagine so," he replied.

"Great. I think so too. Now, what if you told them to step on the second rock, again repeating what you said before? Do you think it might actually take less coaxing the second time?"

"Yes, I would think so," he answered.

"And what if you kept repeating this process, over and over again? Do you see the possibility of getting them to the other side? And throughout it all, you never got angry and never yelled. With every step of the way, their confidence got greater and greater, and they actually fulfilled the potential you saw in them."

Now John was excited. This entire conversation lasted less than two hours and he was ready to get into action. We shook hands and I asked him to call me in two weeks to let me know how it went.

Two weeks later I got an excited phone call from John. He said, "Scott, this has been a fabulous two weeks. I've had some really great conversations with my lawyers. I haven't gotten angry once, haven't yelled, and they are even starting to ask me to go to lunch with them." (Something they used to avoid like the plague.)

"Congratulations!" I said. "Keep up the good work and let me know if you have any problems."

I never heard from him again. I did, however, receive a call about a month after my meeting with John from the chairman in San Francisco. His opening line was, "What did you do to John?"

I had to laugh at the way he asked the question. "What do you mean?" I asked.

"I called down there the other day to find out if anyone had left and spoke to several of the associates. They all said that the problem with John had miraculously been resolved, that he was being wonderful and supportive, and that they were all happy campers."

You can imagine how I felt. Not wanting to tell stories out of school, I simply said, "I knew John was a good guy. You asked me to find out what the problem was, so I did. We put in the correction and that should be the end of that. If you have any other problems, please let me know."

He thanked me profusely and that *was* the end of that.

I again invite you to consider that there is no "truth" about people. There's only what's true for you. People have the ability to be everything from wonderful to awful. You could say they are pure potential. If you give yourself permission to judge and assess them, you'll see all of your judgments and assessments. But if you decide in advance that all people are brilliant, gorgeous, talented, and fabulous, and go looking for the gold, then that's what you will see far more often. Are you beginning to understand why I keep saying: A or B? It's amazing how simple this is!

Back-Story Truism #2: People "show up" around you based on who you believe them to be.

This truism may be tougher to appreciate right away, but consider this: Do you notice that around some people you act one way and around others you act completely different? Haven't you had discussions with someone about a third person you both knew and found that the other party's opinion and impression of the third person was so different from yours that you could hardly believe you were talking about the same person?

This occurs because of Truism #2. We do not live in a vacuum. The beliefs people have about us (which live in their conversations about us) influence who we are around them in dramatic and amazing ways. For me, when I'm around clients who think I'm brilliant, I find myself saying the most brilliant things. Yet around people who, for one reason or another, have judgments about me, I find myself being consistent with their judgments and far from being brilliant.

For example, being patient is not one of my strengths. In fact, I have an extraordinary capability to be impatient. I'm aware of this and work very hard at being patient. Because of my awareness, I'm far more patient than I've ever been.

When I'm around people who know me well, who have no judgments about my behavior, and who don't make me wrong about how I act, I actually find myself being much more peaceful and almost amazingly patient. But once in awhile, when I meet someone new who sees some behavior that they interpret as impatient, I start becoming impatient. As their judgment of me increases, I become for them an increasingly impatient person. It's like a snowball rolling down hill. And what's worse, I see my own behavior and find myself incapable of stopping it.

Psychologists verify this principle. For example, if there is a "problem child" in a family, the old school was to send the child to the psychologist. But they found that as long as the family related to the child as a "problem," then that's how the child continued to be. Today, many psychologists will work instead with the entire family. Once they all agree to stop relating to the child as a "problem" and to start relating to him or her as some version of brilliant, gorgeous, talented and fabulous, more often than not, the problem goes away.

A coach once told me a story which again clearly demonstrates this truism about a company she worked with that did work for the Defense Department of the United States government. The company's main contact in the government was an army general. For the people in the company who worked with him, the relationship was a nightmare. They thought he was a "wall" they had to hurdle for every procurement. They had nothing nice to say about him. To them, he was a roadblock and a "problem." They hired the coach to help them deal with him.

The coaching was not what they expected. She got all the people together who had anything to do with the general and said to them, "I invite you to try an experiment for one month. If it doesn't work, we'll try something different, but here's what I want you to do. For the next month, I request that you change your conversation about the general. Let's make believe that this general is not a problem and that he doesn't enjoy making your life miserable. Let's further make believe that he is a wonderful man, that he deeply loves his country, and that all he thinks about is doing the very best job he knows how to make sure the interests of the government he so much loves are served. Let's also make believe he wants to work with you just as much as you want to work with him, that he likes you and your company, that he believes what you do is good for the country, and that his only reservation in any deal is that the country's interests are served."

Her words were a hard sell because none of what she said reflected their experience of the general. But she convinced them to give it a try for a month, with one condition: They really had to take it on. No faking it. They had to take on her description totally and without reservation and play it out fully for one month. They agreed. They even agreed to have fun doing it.

She left and didn't come back or have any contact with them for the month. When she returned to the company and brought the team together, they all said, almost in unison, "What did you do to the general?"

"What do you mean?" she replied.

"You got to the general, didn't you?" they asked.

"Absolutely not!" she said. "What makes you think that?"

"He's been fabulous. He's working with us and cooperating. We got through several bids without incident. It's been like night and day."

Back-Story Truism #2 at work: People "show up" around you based on who you believe them to be in your conversation about them.

What an advantage you could have and what a powerful and effective leader you could be if you fully embraced this distinction and took responsibility for these two truisms.

Back-Story Truism #3: Who people are and how they behave are separate and distinct.

We create a lot of mischief when we don't honor this truism. What I suggest, as I've said before, is that inside everyone is a bar of solid gold that is often covered up with behaviors based on decisions made a long time ago, ineffective strategies designed to accomplish legitimate results.

Rather than speaking to only the person's behavior while acknowledging that they are, in reality, a decent human being, we collapse the two and speak as if their behavior is who they are.

In my experience, parents do this frequently with their children with damaging results. On a recent business trip I saw an incident that demonstrates this truism. I was sitting outside a gate at the Dallas-Fort Worth airport waiting for a connection that was running late. People filled the waiting area, including a young couple and their five-year-old daughter.

Most of us were reading, relaxing or talking to each other, but not the little girl. She was a beehive of activity. Her father, thinking she was annoying people, tried to make her relax, with little success. I wanted to say to him: "It's all right. She's just being a five-year-old and doing what a five-year-old does. You can't expect her to sit and read USA Today!" I didn't. In hindsight, I'm sorry for that.

Here's what happened next: In his final attempt to get her to stop what she was doing, he called her over and said, "I'm sorry but the plane will be here shortly and you will not be permitted to get on." Not understanding, she looked at her father and asked, "Why not?" His answer was, "They only allow good little girls on the plane."

She slumped down on the floor and began to cry. He had finally accomplished his objective, but at what price? Rather than speaking only about her behavior and honoring her as a human being, he labeled her "bad." Don't we do this all the time?

Had he understood Truism #3, he might have said something like: "You are a fabulous, wonderful, playful, joyous little girl and I love you deeply. I appreciate how much you love to play and have fun. However, there are times when your playfulness can be disruptive to people who have other things to do. This may be one of those times. Many people in this small area waiting for this plane are reading, others conversing. I would appreciate it if you would, just for a few minutes, tone down your playfulness so that you don't disturb anyone. Would you be willing to do that?" Or, better yet, he could have said nothing and just let her be five years old. She really wasn't bothering any of us.

The failure to notice this truism plays out every day at work. We label people lazy, inconsiderate, uncommitted, and on and on, rather than honoring the fundamental goodness in people and focusing our criticisms and concerns on their behavior. As leaders, we need to understand and operate consistently with this truism.

Back-Story Truism #4: *There's nobody "out there" other than a reflection of you.*

I have come to believe that every single person who enters our lives serves as an opportunity to discover who we are. Another way of saying this is that every relationship, no matter how brief or intimate, teaches us something, and the person is our teacher.

It's like each person holds up a mirror so we can see who *we* are. Are we being gracious, loving and accepting, or are we being judgmental, critical and fault-finding? Are we seeing the gold or the dirt? When we see people we like, we are seeing in them those parts of ourselves that we like and are at peace with. But when we see people we don't like, we are seeing in them our own shortcomings, those parts of ourselves that we do not accept or are not at peace with.

As we will discuss later, when we are upset with people, it's never about them. People upset us because they do not fulfill our expectations of them, they are not the way we want them to be, they do not act the way we want them to act, or they do not produce the results we want them to produce.

This may not make sense to you or you may think it is ridiculous. I assure you that this truism, if you are willing to follow it, will serve you well on your path to becoming the leader we are creating.

A Personal Detour

Here's one last example. Are you married? If not, are you living with someone? Do you have a significant other in your life? The statistics regarding personal relationships are disturbing. There is a high probability that you are either unhappy in that relationship now or you will soon be unhappy, separated or divorced! The divorce rate is about 50% among first marriages, 60% among second marriages and 70% among third marriages. The majority of people who do stay together aren't necessarily thrilled with their relationship.

Why is this? Are people not compatible? Do they not know how to get along? In the vast majority of cases, people don't "invent" who their partner is. Rather, people get into personal relationships and do exactly what I have been explaining in this book. They have a picture of the way they think or would like their partner to be. Then they constantly judge and assess who that person is to see if he or she is fitting that picture. On those rare occurrences when the partner does fit, they are happy. Unfortunately, far too often the other person doesn't fit. The cycle of the relationship's destruction begins as disappointments mount one upon the other.

When problems occur, the parties don't honor Truism #3 and speak only of the other person's behavior. They all too frequently attack and make accusations about who the person is, which damages them as much as the comment the father made to the five-year-old damaged her.

By not appreciating Truism #4, partners in a relationship don't treat the other as his or her teacher, nor do they realize that the other person provides them with an opportunity to become a more accepting, gracious, compassionate and loving human being.

Would you like to stack the odds in your favor? Would you like to live happily ever after? It's really fairly simple. Stop judging your partner. Decide he or she is "the one." Invent the other person as brilliant, gorgeous, talented and fabulous. Look for the gold. Not only will that be what you see far more often than not (Truism #1 in action), but also he or she will become more brilliant, more gorgeous, and more fabulous every day (Truism #2 in action).

Time to Take Stock

What new ideas are opening up for you? What are you learning about you and your organization? Are you judging the people who work for you or are you looking for the gold and inventing them as being brilliant, gorgeous, talented and fabulous? What about them? Are they judging each other, making each other wrong and being critical of each other, or are they inventing each other as being brilliant, gorgeous, talented and fabulous? What about your salespeople? Do they make judgments and assessments and opinions about your customers or are they inventing them? I'd venture to guess that the former is the case in each scenario.

Can you see the limitations in that way of being? If you think your boss, your co-worker, your employee or your customer is a jerk, then guess how he or she will show up? What's the likelihood you'll make the sale or get your point across when you're speaking to a jerk?

Consider the possibility that you have had far more control over the quality of your life and the quality of your relationships than you ever imagined. Consider the possibility that your satisfaction and your happiness have always been under your control and you never realized it. What an incredible opportunity you have to be satisfied, happy and surrounded by brilliant, gorgeous, talented and fabulous people.

How do you accomplish that? Remember that it's all about those two conversations, the one from your higher consciousness and the one from your ego and which one you listen to at any given moment. You live in one conversation or the other, you project that conversation onto the world, and then you live in it as if it were the truth. That's the way it is.

Now the question is, "Will you be at the effect of a conversation you created long ago without much thought or consideration, that your ego has kept alive, or will you take responsibility for that conversation and create a world for yourself worth living in?

An old Cherokee Indian story demonstrates this choice:

One evening an old Cherokee told his grandson about a battle that goes on inside people. He said, "My son, the battle is between two 'wolves' inside each of us.

"One is Evil. It is anger, envy, jealousy, sorrow, regret, greed, arrogance, self-pity, guilt, resentment, inferiority, lies, false pride, superiority and ego.

"The other is Good. It is joy, peace, love, hope, serenity, humility, kindness, benevolence, empathy, generosity, truth, compassion and faith."

The grandson thought about it for a minute and then asked his grandfather: "Which wolf wins?"

The old Cherokee replied, "The one you feed."

Speak It and Create It

Your tongue is like a paintbrush. Every time you open your mouth, you paint a picture for yourself and everybody around you to live in. As humans, we are usually unconscious of what comes out of our mouths. I'm asking you to stop that. Wake up. Listen to your thoughts and to the words you say. Decide in advance what you will say about everything and everybody. Then start saying that! It will change your world, your life, and the world and lives of all the people around you. Best of all, doing so will put you on the path to being a twenty-first century leader.

In 1997 I got inspired to take these concepts seriously. I started a new document in my computer and titled it "My Highest Vision." Over the next year I created a picture, in words, of exactly who I would be if I were living in accordance with my highest and best vision for myself. I created the conversation I would live in as if it were the truth. It included everything about who I would be, how I would act, what I would do, where I would live, what my relationships would be like, how I would feel, who people would be for me, my place in the world, the contribution I would be making, what my company would be like and a lot more.

Every morning, I carefully read my new document and committed myself to living that day consistent with my vision. At the end of the day, I reviewed the day's events to see how I did. Each day I learned what I needed to work on and I worked on it. It was the most useful exercise I have ever undertaken. While I am not yet living my life in accordance with every aspect of my highest vision, I've come a long way. I invite you to do the same. If you would like a copy of my document to see what it looks like and to get you started, e-mail me at scott@ thpalliance.com and I'll send it to you.

Summary and Unshackled Leadership Action Items

A number of back-story truisms impact our relationships with the people in our lives. We are mostly unaware of them even though they are just as much truisms as gravity. If you are to become effective as a leader, you must both understand and embrace these truisms:

- *You will always find what you go looking for.*
- *People "show up" around you based on who you believe them to be.*
- *Who people are and how they behave are separate and distinct.*
- *There's nobody "out there" other than a reflection of you.*

1. Begin to notice the degree to which you have judgments and opinions about the people in your company and in your life.

2. Then start noticing the degree to which everyone around you does the same thing. Again, transformation begins by noticing what is actually going on.

3. Take one person in your life who you are having a difficult time with, notice your judgments about them, and then let those judgments go completely. Start "inventing" them as brilliant, gorgeous, talented and fabulous or whatever other empowering words work for you. See if this exercise shifts your relationship with that person.

4. If you are successful in implementing item 3, and I suggest you will be, continue the same process with each of the key people in your life, one at a time.

Sometimes if both people are willing to listen carefully, it is possible to do more than exchange greetings and good wishes. Even to do more than exchange information. The two people may even find out something which neither of them knew before.
&. Gregory Bateson

Chapter 9

Cause and Effect

Let's now take our discussion to a higher level. Consider the possibility that not only will your experience of life and your company be a function of your conversation, but that what you will actually *have* in your life and your company will also be a function of that conversation. Wouldn't that be exciting? To know that you could steer your life and your company in the direction of your dreams with your conversation. Sound too good to be true? Read on.

In the existing paradigm, many if not most people feel as if they have no control or impact over what happens in their lives and in their companies. Yes, you can *say* you're satisfied, and you can *say* you're happy, and you can *say* you relate to all people as if they are beautiful, gorgeous, talented and fabulous but in the final analysis you get what you get. At least that's what these people think.

In Chapter 1 I explained that you and I were born into a paradigm with an already existing set of beliefs and that we bought into all of them without any thought about their validity or usefulness. Even worse, the vast majority of things we were trained to believe either aren't the truth or aren't useful, like driving in Chicago with a street map of Detroit.

With so many "myths" filling the existing paradigm, it amazes me that we get anything done. Let's look at them.

In Chapter 8, I discussed the real estate company I did a project for back in the late 1980s with my associate Amba Gale. I didn't mention then why we got the contract.

It happened this way. I got into a discussion with the senior VP who ultimately hired us. He had a problem he couldn't figure out how to solve. Because many people wanted into the real estate industry, they developed a three-month, fast start program. Agent candidates were immersed in all factors of the real estate business, were taught everything they needed to know to be successful and were coached on how to obtain their license, which virtually everyone received.

As I heard him relate the story, I could almost anticipate what was coming next, and I wasn't surprised at what I heard. One year after the agents got their licenses, for every 100 graduates, 10 were doing very well and 35 had quit the business. The remaining 55 were not doing so badly they had to drop out of the business but they were not doing so great either.

How could that be? They were all taught the same thing. I explained that he had bought into...

Myth: If you know the "right" things to do and do them you'll be successful.

The vast majority of people believe that statement. That's why almost every program you attend and every book you read gives you the supposed formula for success, the five steps or the six practices. Next time you go to a convention or receive a flyer for a seminar, notice that they say, "In this program, you will learn how to…(do this or that) because if you learn the right thing to do and do it you'll surely be successful." It's not the truth. It's a myth.

I graduated from the City University of New York with a degree in electrical engineering. I got a job in Washington, DC with the US Patent and Trademark Office and spent the next four years working as a patent examiner while I went to George Washington University law school at night. I graduated in the top ten percent of my class and moved to California to start a career as an intellectual property attorney having all of the background one would need to be successful in that field. And, from the facts just described, I was obviously smart and well trained.

But as I explained previously, I awoke one day eleven years later to find myself in a solo law practice, struggling to keep busy, living from month to month.

How could that be? I had bought into…

Myth: How smart you are determines your success.

It's a total a myth. Do you know people that are really smart that aren't very successful? Of course you do. Do you know people that aren't very smart at all and who are really successful? Yes.

In the 1970s, the Andrew Carnegie Foundation funded the largest research study ever done to determine what makes a successful individual. They surveyed more than three hundred thousand people in four employment sectors - business, industry, education and government.

The findings speak for themselves. It was found that only 7% of your success is determined by the knowledge you have and only 12% by the skills you possess.

As for me, it wasn't the case that I was lazy or that I didn't try to be successful. I was out there hustling for business all the time. It never seemed to make a difference.

How could that be? I had bought into...

Myth: If you work really hard you'll be successful.

Another myth. Your success has very little to do with how hard you work. The punch line here is not: work smart not hard. People who work the hardest, laborers, are often the least successful. Very often, people who hardly work at all are the most successful.

There are lots of other myths. I'll list some of them but I'll bet you can think of others that you've been told determine your success which have no basis in fact.

Myth: Some people are just lucky.

Myth: It's about being in the right place at the right time.

Myth: It's not who you are, it's who you know.

If all of these "beliefs" are myths, what's the truth? Until it's proven otherwise, here's what I believe:

A fundamental law of the universe is called the law of cause and effect. It means that for every effect there's a cause. For every result, there's a cause. However, because of all of the myths, all of the things we've been told that are simply not true, we look for the wrong causes for the results we produce, both individually and in our organizations.

If we really understand the law of cause and effect, it can be summarized in the form of a formula:

$$T \rightarrow F \rightarrow A = R$$

In other words, we as human beings are fundamentally thinking beings. That's the "T" in the equation. And how we think determines how we feel. That's the "F" in the equation. When I was a lot younger, I wondered which came first, thoughts or feelings. Do we think the way we think because of how we feel or do we feel the way we feel because of the way we think. I'm now convinced it is the later case.

We, these thinking/feeling human beings, go into the world and take action. That's the "A" in the equation. We produce results, the "R" in the equation. If the equation is accurate, which I assert it is, what's the source of the results? It all starts with how we think.

Here's the sad reality: in the existing paradigm, about 90% of the people on this planet are programmed to think in ways that guarantee they will never be successful, which is why they're not. The Small Business Administration keeps statistics on how many companies start each year and how many of them fail within the first 5–10 years. Consistently, 90% that start fail. Notice the correlation?

People who are successful, and I'm primarily talking about those who are financially successful, think differently from people who are unsuccessful. People who run companies successfully think differently from people whose companies fail. That is the bottom line. It's why everything in this book is designed to get you to think differently from the way you may have thought in the past.

Ever since Napoleon Hill wrote *Think and Grow Rich,* and maybe even before then, people have discussed the possibility that our thoughts attract the circumstances into our lives. In his book *You'll See It When You Believe It* (Harper Collins, 2001), the prolific author Dr. Wayne W. Dyer says that what you have in your life is a reflection of your beliefs. This notion has been popularized under the term "the power of positive thinking," the implication being that if you think "positive," you'll have a "positive" experience and produce "positive" results.

For many people, this was a "good idea" until Albert Einstein came along with theories that gave birth to what is now known as quantum physics. In the time between now and the earlier version of this book, an enormous body of information has emerged from quantum physicists about the nature of the universe, far too much to discuss in detail here. As I understand it, Einstein said that the basic "stuff" of the universe is pure energy. So the computer I'm writing this on is energy which has been manifested as a computer. The book you are reading is energy which has been manifested as a book. And you can similarly conclude that about everything else in the physical universe, including you.

You are pure energy manifested as a body. It's an interesting way of thinking about who you are. What's the nature of energy? It's a vibration. If you hooked up an oscilloscope to the electrical outlet in your house, what you would see is a wave vibrating at a particular frequency. In the US, it would be 60 cycles per second, in Europe, 120 cps.

That's the nature of everything, including you. You are fundamentally energy vibrating at a particular frequency.

Now the plot thickens. What determines the frequency at which your energy vibrates? Here's a chart based on the findings of quantum physics:

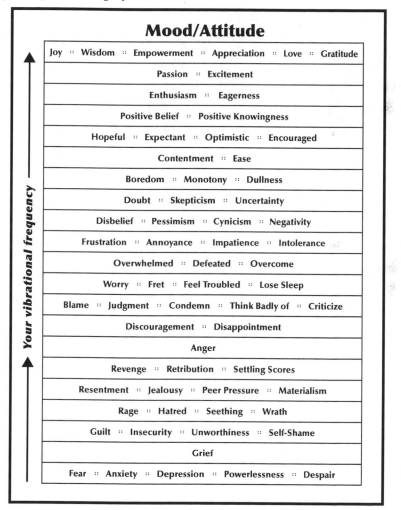

Mood/Attitude

Your vibrational frequency

| Joy :: Wisdom :: Empowerment :: Appreciation :: Love :: Gratitude |
| Passion :: Excitement |
| Enthusiasm :: Eagerness |
| Positive Belief :: Positive Knowingness |
| Hopeful :: Expectant :: Optimistic :: Encouraged |
| Contentment :: Ease |
| Boredom :: Monotony :: Dullness |
| Doubt :: Skepticism :: Uncertainty |
| Disbelief :: Pessimism :: Cynicism :: Negativity |
| Frustration :: Annoyance :: Impatience :: Intolerance |
| Overwhelmed :: Defeated :: Overcome |
| Worry :: Fret :: Feel Troubled :: Lose Sleep |
| Blame :: Judgment :: Condemn :: Think Badly of :: Criticize |
| Discouragement :: Disappointment |
| Anger |
| Revenge :: Retribution :: Settling Scores |
| Resentment :: Jealousy :: Peer Pressure :: Materialism |
| Rage :: Hatred :: Seething :: Wrath |
| Guilt :: Insecurity :: Unworthiness :: Self-Shame |
| Grief |
| Fear :: Anxiety :: Depression :: Powerlessness :: Despair |

This is extraordinary. As your mood, your attitudes and your feelings, move up the scale from fear, through anger, then pessimism, to hopefulness and enthusiasm to love, gratitude, joy and appreciation, the frequency at which the you that is you vibrates increases.

Here's the best part. Since you are fundamentally energy and everything else in the physical universe is also energy, the energy that you are interacts with the rest of the energy and you attract to you that which is consistent with the energy that you are and repel from you that which is inconsistent with the energy you are. That's the law of cause and effect.

Think of yourself as being like a magnet. We attract things to ourselves that are consistent with our feelings/mood/attitude (for me, those are all the same thing). It's your thinking that ultimately determines how you feel.

If you want a more rigorous discussion of cause and effect than presented here, as well as the work of the quantum physicists, read *Quantum Physics, Illusion or Reality* by Alastair Rae, (Cambridge University Press, 1986), or *Quantum Legacy, The Discovery That Changed Our Universe,* by Barry Parker (Prometheus Books, 2002).

If you like watching movies and want to see some amazing explanations of this, order these three from amazon. com: *What the Bleep do we Know, What the Bleep — Down the Rabbit Hole,* and *The Secret* by Rhonda Burns. The latter movie created quite a stir when it arrived on the scene in early 2007. Larry King, Oprah, Ellen DeGeneres, Montel Williams and others featured it. Like most controversial films, those unwilling to believe the simplicity of this explanation of the law of cause and effect greeted them with enormous skepticism. I suggest you watch all of those movies and decide for yourself.

It's exciting for me that Napoleon Hill's insights are now topics of daily discussion. While I've explored the law of cause and effect only recently, I have understood its effect since I started coaching 23 years ago. It has been the basis of all of the work we've done in organizations since then.

You Get What You Feel

Returning to our discussion about satisfaction, if you spend your days being satisfied and generating satisfaction in your conversation, then you will attract into your life circumstances and events that contribute to your satisfaction. Pretty great!

However, the converse is equally true. If you spend your days being dissatisfied and generating dissatisfaction in your conversation, then you will attract into your life circumstances and events that contribute to your dissatisfaction. The law of cause and effect is totally neutral. It doesn't care what you generate. It just responds.

The same applies to happiness. If you spend your days choosing to be happy and generating happiness in your conversation, then you will attract circumstances and events into your life that contribute to your happiness. Also pretty great!

The converse is true here too. If you spend your days choosing to be unhappy and generating unhappiness in your conversation, then you will attract into your life circumstances and events that contribute to your unhappiness.

In 2005, we worked with a company whose equity, after 10 years of operation, was in the red. Being an energy detective,

I set out to look for the reason. It didn't take long to find it. I asked the president of the company if he was satisfied with his company or not. His answer was: "I'm never satisfied!"

So I asked why? His answer: "Because I always think we can do better today than we did yesterday and we can do better tomorrow than we did today." Then I asked one of his salespeople what typically happens when he comes back from calling on a couple of customers. He said that if he happens to call on two customers, the president will typically ask him how come he didn't call on a third. If he called on three, he'll be asked how come he didn't call on a fourth. Nothing was ever good enough.

Finally, I asked him if there were ever celebrations in the company. When you come back with a nice juicy order, does the president celebrate your success? His answer was a quick "are you kidding. In fact, he would frequently say, come on, you can do better than that."

This president was never satisfied and never happy. In fact, he was consistently dissatisfied and unhappy. The law of cause and effect has no sense of humor. It's totally neutral. It just responds. So he created a company to support him in being dissatisfied and unhappy. Needless to say, when I told him he was the reason why they were consistently unprofitable, he wasn't too thrilled.

This law of cause and effect applies in every area. If you think people are jerks, guess what you'll attract? Jerks! But if you think people are brilliant, gorgeous, talented and fabulous, you'll attract brilliant, gorgeous, talented and fabulous people. Not only does your thinking and your speaking influence and/ or create the way the world occurs for you, it also *creates* how your world ultimately will be.

Here's a powerful way to relate to what I'm saying:

You can't get anyplace other than where you start!

You can't get to satisfaction from dissatisfaction. If you're dissatisfied, you will attract into your life events and circumstances that contribute to your dissatisfaction. If you want to get to satisfaction you have to start from satisfaction. It may sound crazy, but it's true. You can't be unhappy and hope to be happy one day. You have to start from being happy.

Another way of saying this is that what you do doesn't matter. It's who you are "being" that counts. Be satisfied, be happy, be enthusiastic, be positive, be loving, be joyous and watch your world mirror those ways of being.

Can you now understand why I said what I did in Chapter 1, that I have noticed a common theme among all successful companies: they consist of a group of enthusiastic, confident, optimistic, appreciative and happy people who work together on behalf of a future they have all committed themselves to? Can you now understand why I truly believe that this is the formula for success? If you have a group of enthusiastic, confident, optimistic, appreciative and happy people in your company, they will attract to the company opportunities and circumstances that contribute to that attitude. If everyone in your company is focused on a clearly identified future they have all committed themselves to, they will attract to the company all of the necessary circumstances that will contribute to that future becoming a reality!

Remember the 1970 Andrew Carnegie Foundation research study I referred to earlier in this chapter? It was found that only 7% of your success is determined by the knowledge you have and only 12% by the skills you possess. The biggest revelation was that a whopping 81% of your success is determined by your attitude!

Extraordinary! Maybe strategic planning isn't the most important thing for you to pay attention to after all. Same with all that emphasis on cost cutting, right sizing, down sizing, efficiency and all the other buzz words and popular fads. Just maybe the key to your success is to create an environment where people can be enthusiastic, confident, optimistic, appreciative and happy and create a future they can all be excited about and committed to.

Is all I've revealed thus far "the truth?" My best answer is that it's totally consistent with our experience working with people for over 23 years, and I invite you to find out for yourself.

Summary and Unshackled Leadership Action Items

Whether we realize it or not, whether we understand it or not, quantum physics is proving that we live in a world of cause and effect. Our thinking creates our feelings and emotions and those feelings and emotions determine what we attract into our lives and our companies. You can't get anyplace other than where you start from. Therefore you have to choose your attitude, not wait for it to come from your circumstances.

1. Study the mood/attitude/vibrational frequency chart above. What is your most predominant attitude?

2. Can you see that the circumstances in your life and your business are a complete match for that attitude?

3. Are you willing to consider that your attitude is the source of your circumstances rather than vice versa?

4. Practice moving your mood/attitude up the chart one step at a time. Realistically, you can't get from discouragement and disappointment to love, gratitude, appreciation and joy overnight. But you could, with a bit of focus, get to skepticism and uncertainty. Once there, with some more focus, you could get to pessimism and doubt and eventually to hopefulness and optimism. Just reach for the next best feeling and keep doing that until you generate feelings of excitement, appreciation and joy. It's not impossible. It takes commitment, work and focus but the effort is worth every step of the journey.

Security is mostly a superstition. It does not exist in nature. Nor do the children of men as a whole experience it. Avoiding danger is no safer in the long run than outright exposure.

Life is either a daring adventure or nothing.
❦ Helen Keller

*Step 8: Distinguish the
predominant world paradigm
of fear and scarcity*

Chapter 10

Fear and Scarcity

Here's another profound consequence of not appreciating the law of cause and effect. If you look into our Western culture, what do you identify as the predominant human emotion? Sadness, happiness, joy, frustration, anger? When I ask people this question, under any circumstances, it rarely takes longer than five seconds for someone to answer *fear.*

And fear it is! Fear is the most prevalent of human emotions. In fact, the book *A Course in Miracles,* and many other scholarly works, say that there are only two human emotions: love and fear. Anything that isn't love is fear. Regardless of whether this is true, consider that, at the very least, fear is a very common human emotion.

If this is true, and I assert that it is, why is fear the most prevalent of human emotions? I hope by now you are beginning to be able to answer these questions for yourself: it's the conversation of the ego. The ego tells you that the world is a scary place and you had better beware. This is just one of the many ways it keeps you off balance and not able to hear the conversation of your higher consciousness.

What's the opposite of fear? We've already established that it's "love," but let's look at it from a more practical perspective. My favorite words that express the opposite of fear are *faith, trust* and *optimism.* If we define fear as the expectation of an unfavorable or undesirable outcome, then faith, trust and optimism all point to the expectation of a favorable or desirable outcome.

The fact that we live in a fear-based culture is so much a part of our paradigm that when we see or experience people who are overly happy, enthusiastic and optimistic, we often call them a "Pollyanna" or naïve. We reason that since they think the world is wonderful, they certainly can't be in touch with "reality." Why do we call optimistic people a "Pollyanna"? Because fear is the biggest game in town — we just don't go around talking about it or admitting it. It's like water to the fish.

But it's important to bring fear up to the surface. If you "come from" a place of fear, meaning that you are fearful about something, then that is what you will project onto the world you live in and that is what you will see. Regardless of the real scariness or safety of any situation, if you believe there is something to fear, that's what your experience will be.

Haven't you encountered people who are afraid of something you consider to be totally safe? You may not be able to understand why they are afraid of it, but they are. It's their belief and to them it's the truth.

For example, as a bicycling enthusiast I go on many bicycle trips. Often I have to climb long, steep hills. What keeps me going on those long up hills is the knowledge that sooner or later there will be a downhill... and I love those down hills. The steeper they are and the faster I can go, the better.

However, I have ridden with many riders who, on those down hills, hold onto their brakes for dear life and descend very slowly. They believe going fast isn't safe. For me, it's safer to go fast than to hold onto your brakes. I also think they're missing all the fun. However, going fast isn't fun for them; it's scary.

The same is true with the bear in the woods. When some people encounter a bear, they pass out from fright. For me and others, it's an exciting experience.

Fear, like everything else, is an interpretation of existing circumstances. It's an expectation, whether real or not, of an unfavorable outcome. To the fearful person, it's very real.

Here's the kicker. Given the law of cause and effect, if you are fearful, you will attract into your life and your company events and circumstances that support your fear. Remember, fear isn't bad; it's like everything else in life. Its only use is to attract more of itself. If you want to have a lot of things in your life that generate fear in you, be fearful!

Conversely, if you are optimistic, you will attract into your life and your company events and circumstances that support you in experiencing optimism. Optimism isn't *better* than fear; it just brings different consequences. The good news is that you have the ability to choose whether you're fearful or optimistic, for both fear and optimism are decisions you make.

Once again, A or B. Faith, optimism, trust, joy, peace and happiness are all conversations emanating from your higher consciousness. Fear is the main conversation emanating from your ego. Remember, your ego is all about survival. It wants to keep you in your comfort zone. Every time you think of venturing out of that zone, the ego responds with, "Watch out."

Remember the law firm I worked with in San Francisco, where I was asked to "do something" with the angry manager of the Los Angeles office? They are a great example of this distinction. The firm had grown rapidly and extensively from its beginnings in 1975 up to and through 1990. Then something happened and the growth suddenly stopped. When I was contacted in 1996, it was on the verge of a decline.

The management team contacted me to facilitate a strategic planning retreat to plot a course to get them back on track. When I agreed, I insisted on interviewing as many of the partners as possible, particularly those who were at the firm since the beginning, so I could isolate the problem.

What I learned was fascinating. Everyone told me that during the growth years, the firm's "leader" (whom I'll call Larry), was the most optimistic, the most positive and the most encouraging person you could ever imagine meeting. His philosophy was to have fun, do good work, take care of the clients and let success take care of itself. The firm never did any marketing; they just did what Larry said. They had lots of fun, they did the best job they could do for their clients, and most important, they never worried. Why? Because Larry told them not to.

One of the firm's partners (whom I'll call Paul), told me a particularly telling story. The firm specialized in litigating very large cases and it wasn't atypical for a team of lawyers to work on a single case full-time. Paul was part of a team of five lawyers who had worked for several years on one multi-million dollar case. One day the case settled leaving the five lawyers with no work and with no obvious source of new work.

Paul went to Larry and asked, "What do we do now?"

As was typical for Larry, his response was, "Don't worry about it. You five have been working hard for a number of years. You've earned a break. Tell your team to take some time off and have fun. I guarantee you it won't take long before we'll be screaming to get you back here."

That wasn't what Paul expected to hear because he was worried they'd all be laid off. But Paul was a young attorney, and if Larry said not to worry, who was he to do otherwise? Paul and his team took off on a fully paid sabbatical. Less than thirty days later a new case came in and Paul and his team were back at it.

I heard story after story that replicated Paul's. The mood of the firm was one of faith, trust and optimism, because that's the kind of leader Larry was. As a result, the firm grew and grew and grew. It's a great example of the law of cause and effect operating in all its glory.

So what happened? Well, one day in 1990, Larry woke up and looked at what he had created. He had hundreds of people working in the firm, with a payroll in the tens of millions of dollars. He got scared. He related to the group and me at this strategic planning retreat that up until that fateful day he was confident of the firm's ability to thrive. But for some reason, on that day, he awoke and said, "Oh my God. We have most of our work coming from one client. They have been able to send us big cases for 15 years, but can it continue?" He started to doubt. Fear set in. And the rest got ugly.

The day after that realization, Larry gathered his partners and expressed his concerns. He said that they had to market, diversify and look for new clients; it wasn't good that they had all their eggs in one basket. Unfortunately, Larry's partners didn't know what to make of this. They didn't want to market. They never had and didn't know how. Everyone had a different opinion about what they should do. They started to argue, bicker and make each other wrong. The teamwork went out the window, taking all the wind out of their sails. In the face of their confusion, the results turned to confusion.

Happily, this story had a wonderful ending. We got what happened out on the table during the strategic planning retreat. We followed it up with several multi-day partner retreats to "clean up" all the upsets, disappointments and frustrations that occurred during those six rocky years. In the end, everyone committed to get back to what inspired their success: (i.e. having fun, taking care of the clients, doing good work, and being optimistic about the future.) The last I heard, the firm was breaking growth records.

Here's another more recent example. In 2005 I was invited to work with a company whose sales had been flat at between $40 and $50 million for five straight years, with very little profitability. Again, being the "mood" detective that I am, I interviewed many people in the company to determine the source of this situation.

It didn't take long for me to find out that the owner of the company was a worrier. His wife told me that he would wake up in the middle of the night worrying about his company. He had in fact told people that he wanted his managers to worry about his company.

Take a look at the chart in Chapter 9. Worry and losing sleep are particular vibrations. They are just a kinder, gentler version of fear.

We took the owner and the management team away for a three-day retreat and took them through every chapter of this book, focusing on the law of cause and effect and how it was impacting their company's performance. They left the retreat with a commitment to stop worrying and start generating excitement, enthusiasm, optimism and faith. They aligned on a vision for the future of the company and took a stand for being a $150 million company in five years. They further committed to listen for possibility and trust that with their new focus the future they committed to would become a reality.

Now remember, their sales had been flat for five years so this was all pretty bold. But when the energy shifts, anything and everything becomes possible. What happened? In 2005, they did $67 million, in 2006 they did $89 million and in 2007 they did $104 million, at a much higher level of profitability. This stuff works!

Scarcity

People are afraid of many things: death, public speaking, failure, success, embarrassment. One fear is so prevalent in our culture yet so unrecognized that it needs special attention. It's a fear that is passed down from generation to generation in a very subtle way.

In speeches and workshops, I frequently ask the attendees: "When you were a child, did your parents tell you to eat all of the food on your plate because there were poor people starving somewhere?" I know my parents told me this. I suspect yours did too. But until I started asking the question, I had no idea that almost everyone received this message. In my programs, almost everyone responds with a "yes." It's often fun to find out where their parents told them the starving people lived. It's usually China or Africa, but sometimes other exotic places.

When you stop to think about it, though, it's bizarre to say that you have to eat all your food because somebody is starving in some far off land. How is your eating your food (or not) going to impact this starving person? Regardless, this is what we hear, and there is a powerful message hidden in these words. The obvious message is that you don't want to waste food. However, what goes along with that is the implication that you don't want to waste food because our planet's resources are limited. Thus we develop a belief in scarcity. Whenever we believe in scarcity, we create a corresponding fear that we won't have enough or that what we have will get used up.

Look at our culture and look into your own life to see if you experience this. Aren't we told that the American game is to work hard, invest, plan for the future, save and accumulate? Don't you spend time doing just that? Don't businesses spend an inordinate amount of time doing strategic planning? Aren't most people investing, gambling, playing the stock market, buying lottery tickets or trying to accumulate as much money as possible?

You might ask, "What's wrong with that?" Nothing is *wrong* with it. However, if you or your company are saving and investing simply because you are coming from a belief in scarcity — a fear that if you don't, either the money will run out or you won't have enough — then there are serious consequences.

When you come from scarcity, money becomes very important. You believe that one day you'll have enough and you'll feel secure. But it never happens. Remember, you can't get to anyplace other than where you start. So if the underlying belief is scarcity, no matter how much you have, it's never enough. No amount of money is ever enough in a paradigm of scarcity. The more you get, the more you want. It's an endless game. You end up being in the game for the money and you end up appearing or actually being greedy.

The events of 2002 show this. Enron, MCI, and Adelphia Cable had fortunes, but not enough to satisfy the key officers. Rampant greed took over. I ask you, once you're a multi-millionaire, how much more do you need? Tens of thousands of people die every day from starvation while corporate executives in the United States earn tens of millions of dollars yearly. While I have no problem with people earning whatever is fair, the paychecks of some executives are way out of proportion, all driven by this paradigm we live in — a paradigm of fear and scarcity.

When you come from scarcity, guess what you attract into your life? Scarcity! This is why the majority of people struggle to make ends meet, often not accomplishing even that.

When you come from both fear and scarcity, guess what you experience in life? Struggle, effort, stress, sleepless nights, and depression. You can't have happiness or satisfaction while stuck in that pattern of thinking.

So many people think they'll one day get to abundance. However, you can't get to abundance with scarcity thinking. Scarcity thinking is useful for one and only one thing: producing scarcity.

Guess who the keeper of the scarcity conversation is? You guessed it, the ego. Your higher consciousness knows that *we live in a universe of infinite abundance and that there is always more than enough to go around.* I'll bet it's hard to read those words, let alone believe them, because the ego's scarcity conversation is so deeply imbedded in our paradigm.

Summary and Unshackled Leadership Action Items

The most predominant human emotions are fear and scarcity. People who are overly optimistic are looked upon as naïve. It's even fashionable to be poor. After all, who would want to be the "filthy rich." However, 90% of the people on the planet have an annual income of $25,000 or less and 3% of the people on the planet control 97% of the wealth. These are all consequences of our thinking.

1. Are you afraid or do you trust? Start to notice. We'll dig more deeply into this in the next chapter. But for now, just start to notice what dominates your conversation: fear, worry, concern, or faith, trust and optimism.
2. What's your attitude about money and wealth? Again, start to notice what dominates your thinking. Do you think that you need to figure out a way to get your piece of a limited pie or do you view your job as making the pie bigger?
3. How concerned are you about the competition? Do you see yourself as competing for a limited amount of business or do you see the world as having plenty to go around? Or someplace in the middle?

Chapter 11

You and Your Company

We have enough cards on the table now, so let's pause for a few moments and reflect on what we've discussed. Doing so will lay the foundation for where we go next.

We will continue to go deeper and deeper into the paradigm we all live in. At each stop along the way, reflect on what you are uncovering about yourself and your company.

Ask yourselves the following questions. Consider each in turn and either write down or reflect on your answers:

What do you see so far about you? Your company?
Where are you personally?
Where do you think your company is?

As you think about the answers to these questions, consider such aspects as happiness, satisfaction, who people are for you and the quality of your relationships.

Realize that nobody lives totally in fear or totally in trust, faith and optimism just as nobody lives totally in scarcity or totally in abundance. So if you create two continuums, one with fear at 0 and trust/faith/optimism at 100, and the other with scarcity at 0 and abundance at 100, what score would you give yourself on each? What score would you give your company? How do you think others in your company would score the organization? Ask them. You might learn something about other people's attitudes or about the mood of the company.

If you didn't give yourself a score of 100 on the fear/optimism continuum, answer these questions:

What are you worrying about?

What happened that initiated that worry?

What impact do those concerns have on your peace of mind?

Is whatever there is in your conversation regarding the world being a scary and/or limited place necessary? Really?

Is it necessary that you be where you are on the continuums?

More important, is this thinking useful? Helpful?

After you've answered these questions, and it's important to answer them honestly before moving on, consider the following:

You are where you are because that's where you've chosen to be. You likely chose sometime long ago, maybe when you were three or four or five years old, maybe based on an attitude or comment your mother or father made. And today you live with that choice without ever re-examining it.

How We Choose Our Messages

When I was very young, I lived in New York City. When I was old enough to go outside and play with my friends on my own, my mother would say as I walked out the door, "Be careful!" She didn't say, "I love you," "Have a great time," or "Have fun," but "Be careful." I didn't know at the time that "Be Careful" was her code for all of the other statements listed above. I do know the impact it had on me. I concluded that there must be something I had to be careful about! I also heard other prescriptions like "Don't talk to strangers." In hindsight that's when I learned there were things and people to be afraid of.

There was also the "eat all the food on your plate" message, which introduced me to the idea of scarcity. I lived most of my life at the low ends of both the fear/optimism and scarcity/abundance continuums. At some level, that's what I chose. At another level, that's what chose me! But those were the choices that used my life.

The great part of being an adult and fully understanding what we have been discussing is the realization that you can always choose again. And again. And again. You're not stuck with the choices you've made in the past unless you choose to stay there. People stay in their old belief systems for many reasons that we will cover later. However, life is a choice and your job, especially as a leader in the new paradigm we are creating, is to choose wisely.

You can see the glass as either half empty or half full. Your choice makes all the difference. You've heard this statement before, but here it takes on new meaning. If you're always seeing what's missing, what you will attract into your life is more of the missing. That's the law of cause and effect in action. But if you always see what's there, if you are grateful and appreciative for what you have rather than complaining about what you don't have, you'll attract into your life more to be grateful for.

The amount of abundance in your life is exactly consistent with your willingness to think abundantly. What materializes in your physical world is simply an out-picturing of what's going on in your internal world.

Too many people think the way to create more abundance is to work harder. Nonsense! Plenty of people work very hard and have very little, just as others hardly work and have a lot. It's not about luck or working smart. You create abundance with your thinking. Do you want to be abundant? Think abundantly. Do you want to be poor? Believe in scarcity.

Pay Attention to Your Mood

How does all of this apply on an organizational level? How do you use this information to be an unshackled leader and have the freedom to experience the extraordinary? An organization is a collection of thinking beings. As a result, it has a collective energy — a mood — that determines what's possible.

If the mood is upbeat, enthusiastic, positive and optimistic, and people are all pulling together, you're going to have great results. Remember the San Francisco law firm I worked with? The mood during those fifteen growth years was extraordinary. So were their results.

However, if people are fearful, selfish, coming from scarcity and not working together, watch out. This is a formula for disaster.

Many years ago a Los Angeles company hired me to coach them. The company was not doing well. As usual, I spent a day at the company and interviewed as many people as possible. What I found was scary. The company president/owner thought that fear was a great motivator, so he used it regularly. During the weekly staff meetings, he would spend most of the time telling people how terrible things were, what poor shape the company was in and how uncertain the financial outlook was. He would end by saying that if they all didn't get to work and produce results he couldn't be sure he could keep the doors open.

He thought that approach would motivate them to work harder. One staff member revealed that she would often go home so depressed that she would drink herself to sleep. People were afraid all the time. Interestingly, fear did not motivate them. Instead it created a mood of gloom and doom, and these words adequately describe their results.

At the end of the interviews, I discussed my findings with the president. Because he felt that fear was a great motivator for him, he assumed it would be a great motivator for others. He didn't consider the negative impact it had on the employees' mood. Ultimately, he agreed to change his ways, and the results started to change soon thereafter.

Set the Right Tone

Again, pause and ask yourself...

What's the truth about your organization?

Is that truth what you're committed to?

Where do you need to go from here?

How do you create the kind of company that makes you happy and proud, and that produces extraordinary results?

As the leader of your organization, you set the company's tone. If you're excited, enthusiastic, optimistic, appreciative and happy, your people will follow suit. Conversely, if you motivate with fear and are negative and pessimistic, your people will be that way too. Being a leader means being conscious of the tone you set.

Setting the right tone is a matter of where you start. Start from where you want to end up. Start from being a happy group of satisfied, turned on, joyous, alive, enthusiastic, optimistic people, having faith in the future, working together, aligned on a vision, with a commitment to support each other in being that way and watch out. Nothing and nobody will be able to interfere with your success.

Summary and Unshackled Leadership Action Items

This chapter actually is a summary of what we've covered so far. It asks the questions and creates the action steps necessary to take off the shackles and be an effective leader. Before going on, re-read the chapter and answer the questions posed.

Chapter 12

The Design of Life

Before we continue on our journey into the existing paradigm, let me assure you that this book is not intended to be a psychological treatise. After all, I'm a coach, not a psychologist. Having said that, this discussion would be incomplete without some mention of why we are the way we are, and more particularly, why we have our attention on ourselves and are concerned with our survival, that is, why our thinking and our lives are dominated by the voice of the ego or why we even have an ego in the first place.

In Chapter 3, we discussed the origins of "the conversation." Then we said that when we are born, for all practical purposes, there existed only the conversation of our higher consciousness. It doesn't stay that way for long. Events happen. Our diaper is wet and we cry. Someone comes right away or doesn't. At any given time, mothers, fathers, sisters, brothers, or grandparents perform many tasks around us.

Soon we grow, mature, and develop a personality. We crawl; we walk; we talk; people react to what we do. We go to school and interact with other children and teachers. The number of events we experience is endless.

In reality, none of these events mean anything of themselves. However, human beings have a hard time believing that events don't mean anything. In fact, we believe just the opposite. We think *everything* means *something*.

Beginning at an early age, we interpret everything that occurs and assign it a meaning. It's important to understand that for us the event does indeed have the meaning we give it, whether fact or not. For us, it is "true."

Then we store the event, with the meaning we gave it, in our consciousness. It doesn't stop there. The next event occurs; we interpret it, give it some meaning, and store it away. We repeat the process again and again and again. Along the way, we make judgments and decisions about ourselves, the world, other people and how we fit in. What emerges is an elaborate story about everything. The entire process — the decisions, the judgments, the story — are all a part of the conversation of our lower mind.

How This Process Shapes Who We Are

Let's add to that process the paradigm in which we were born. In that paradigm, there were and are parents, grandparents, relatives, friends and teachers. I will call that group "adults." What's apparent but not said is that the adults are the ones who *know*. They are the smart ones. They are the ones who have the experience, so they know! The children are the ones who *don't know*. Therein lies the problem. As children, we were treated like we don't know. It doesn't take us long to figure that out.

The adults' job is to teach the children. Unfortunately, very few of our parents went to school to learn how to be a parent. They learned how to parent from watching their parents, who learned from watching theirs. In most instances, but not exclusively, they teach not with love, affection, encouragement and appreciation, but with yelling, punishment, violence, disrespect and abuse. How many children do you think were *not* yelled at, scolded, hit or punished? I suspect very few. If they didn't get the negative messages at home, they got them on the playground, in school or someplace else.

In the face of such negativity, what do you think children decide about themselves? That they're brilliant, gorgeous, talented and fabulous? Hardly. They decide that they must not be very smart, they're not good, something is wrong with them, they're not worthy and they're not lovable. Let me introduce you to the conversations of the ego.

Under these circumstances, as a child matures into an adult, do you think he or she believes "I'm okay" or "I'm not okay"? I suspect your instinct is the same as mine. Not okay! If you dig deeply into the conversation of the ego, it offers three main themes: I'm not worthy, I'm not good enough and I'm not loved! Pretty exciting, huh?

My Story

Growing up, my life wasn't that bad, but it wasn't that great either. I grew up in an apartment in the Bronx, New York, with my mother, father and older sister. On the surface it was your typical American family. But here's what was happening below the surface:

My parents were the kind of people who, when I did what I was supposed to do, said nothing. I don't remember getting any particular acknowledgement or "atta-boys." On the other hand, when I didn't do what I was supposed to do, I heard plenty. I heard the line "wait until your father gets home" a lot.

Predictably, in the face of no acknowledgement for doing things well and lots of criticism for doing things wrong, I decided early on that I must not be very smart. I also questioned whether I was a valuable human being who deserved to be loved (because I didn't feel like I was). I ultimately decided I wasn't a valuable human being. Those were decisions one and two.

My mother, again in my recollection, listened the way I previously described as *what am I going to say next*. So around her I had to work hard to get a word in edgewise. It didn't seem to me that my father wanted to work that hard, so slowly but surely he got quiet. I thought he was being a wimp (my interpretation) and someplace along the way I decided that I'd never let a woman dominate me the way she dominated him. That was decision number three.

My father was a hard working plumber. While we always had a place to live, clothes to wear and food to eat, many times we couldn't do things I wanted to do because we couldn't afford it. Some of our relatives had a lot of money but my father always spoke poorly of them. He blamed them for not helping him out. I made lots of decisions around that. I decided you had to work hard (decision number four), money was in short supply (number five), rich people aren't nice (number six) and we were not one of "them" (number seven). Does any of this sound familiar? Can you relate to any of these decisions?

I could go on and on, but I hope I've made my point. It's difficult, if not impossible in that paradigm, to emerge from childhood with your self-esteem intact, thinking you're okay. My conclusion, after looking at this for twenty some-odd years, is that we all have our version of "I'm not okay."

This Process Impacts Us All

When we do retreats, we like to do a certain exercise with people to end the event. I've always thought the exercise would be a wonderful experience for people, but usually it's not. Here's the exercise: We tell people to close their eyes and we ask them, "What's your gift? What makes you unique? What do you bring to life that's special?"

We then tell people to open their eyes and write down what came to mind as we asked those questions. Next, we ask people to come to the front of the room, one at a time, face their team members and say, "My unique contribution to life is…" I guarantee you we have never had anyone stand up in front of a group and say, "I'm brilliant, gorgeous, talented and fabulous."

Then we have all of their team members tell them what they left out. The person's job is to stand in front of the room and listen to what their fellow employees think of them. In *every* case, the people standing in front of the room are stunned to hear how well their teammates think of them and all of the wonderful attributes their co-workers think they have. Why? People's conversations about themselves are generally so negative and limiting that it's hard for them to hear all the acknowledgements. It's almost painful. In fact, it's not uncommon for people to dismiss what others say, for them to say "enough already," and for them to want the process to be over.

We don't let it end quite yet. At this point, we ask everyone to rise and give the person in the front of the room a standing ovation for about thirty seconds. Now I don't know about you, but I love getting a standing ovation. It makes me feel like I did a good job. But for the typical person, it is painful to stand and be acknowledged that way. Almost every person tries to walk away after a few seconds. We don't let them. They have to stand there and take it.

It sounds unbelievable, but it's true. Try it with your team. You'll see for yourself. People are so used to being criticized and criticizing themselves that to be acknowledged publicly is almost too much to take. We literally get used to the conversation of the ego: I'm not worthy, I'm not good enough, and I'm not loved!

That's why we focus our attention on ourselves and why we're concerned with our survival. When you don't appreciate the truth of whom you are; when you don't live in a conversation where you're brilliant, gorgeous, talented and fabulous; when you actually think something is wrong with you, you focus your attention on yourself. Since it looks to you and me like everybody else is okay and we're the only ones with this problem, we feel adversarial with other people and become concerned with our survival.

In our attempt to "make it" in this paradigm, we hop right on the "ladder of success" and start climbing toward the top. We've learned through the years that success means achieving "The American Dream" — the house with the white picket fence, the Mercedes or BMW in the garage, and the designer clothes.

Here's the cruel joke. We think one day we'll get to the point on the ladder where we have accomplished enough that we will now feel okay. However, this ignores the reality that the ladder rests on a foundation of "not okay." Recall the conversation about satisfaction, which says that you can't get to anyplace other than where you start. In our paradigm, we start from "not okay." Unless we question that belief, every step of the way reinforces that belief.

So you've accumulated all this "stuff" but you still feel "not okay." Instead of questioning the fundamental reason why you're climbing in the first place (because we don't consciously know the reason why), we conclude that we must need more "stuff." So we keep on climbing.

We keep climbing and climbing, all the while concerned with our survival, placing our attention on ourselves, wondering if we'll ever have enough and feeling frustrated that we're not more peaceful and secure. We're convinced that everyone else has it made and that we are in competition with them. In the midst of all that thinking, we're supposed to be happy. However, we're not and that's exactly the way the ego likes it.

In the Lew Epstein clubs we used to have an annual meeting of all of the clubs. Every Memorial Day, men and women would gather at one of the club cities for this wonderful event. We had men's meetings, women's meetings and joint meetings.

One year in the men's meeting, with a couple of hundred men in the room, with Lew and Francine leading the discussion, one man shared what life was like for him. He was a company executive with a lot of responsibilities. He shared that he spent much of his day scared about his responsibilities, that he often second guessed the decisions he made, that he was afraid to let people know about his insecurities because he didn't want them to view him as weak and that he had many sleepless nights where all he could do was replay in his mind all that he had done during the day and question whether he did the "right" things.

I remember sitting in the room totally relating to what he was saying, for he might as well have been speaking for me. I started to feel a bit of relief, realizing there was a least one other person on the planet who had the same insecurities I had. I was amazed by his courage in getting up and sharing what he shared, being certain that the other men in the room likely were judging him and relating to him as weak.

Just then Lew, being the brilliant leader that he was, stopped the man, turned to the rest of us, and simply asked, "For how many of you men is this man speaking on your behalf?" *Every hand went up!* Can you imagine? Every hand went up. I was blown away. I couldn't believe it.

The moment the speaker finished and sat down, my hand shot up. Lew called on me. I stood up, walked to the front of the room, looked at the assembly of men (all of whom *I* thought had their acts together), and asked, "Are you serious? Do every one of you really question whether you're good enough, smart enough, capable enough, like I do?" They all nodded their heads yes!

This was a life-changing moment for me. I realized that I was not in this situation alone, that my conversation about me was not a unique conversation, that it was a conversation in the paradigm I had picked up along the way, and that we were all in this together. That didn't make my conversation about me go away, but at least I knew I wasn't alone and I didn't have to hide out any more. I didn't have to make believe I was okay when I didn't feel like I really was. It was very freeing.

Your Conversation and You

Again it's time to pause. Are you clear yet that you live in a conversation? Think back to the exercise in Chapter 8 where I asked people to list the not-so-nice conversations they have about others and the wonderful things they could say about people. Which of the two do you think most accurately describes your conversation about you?

Are you critical of yourself? Do you second-guess yourself and beat yourself up for the "wrong" decisions you make? Or do you relate to yourself as brilliant, gorgeous, talented and fabulous?

Your answer here is important because as long as you're critical of yourself you'll be critical of others. That's the way it is. To reach your full potential as an unshackled leader, you have to commit to resolving the issues you have with you!

Here's the good news: to the degree you are critical of yourself, it's just the conversation of your ego.

Here's the bad news: to the degree you are critical of yourself, you listen to and think that conversation is the truth. And, you likely think you're the only one who has it.

Rest assured, you're not. We all have it. Part of becoming a conscious human being is to realize that and to move beyond it.

That Lew Epstein International Men's and Women's Club's annual retreat was a life-changing event for me. While I knew intellectually before that day that we all live in this "not okay" conversation, I hadn't let that sink in. That day it did. I finally got it that this is the ego conversation and that it isn't personal to me. One of my coaches used to say that if you walk outside into a rainstorm, you would get wet, yet you wouldn't think it was a personal rainstorm.

In fact, the rainstorm is a great metaphor. We are all living in this rainstorm and getting wet, yet we take it personally. It's time to stop doing that. It's time to take a stand for your worth and value. It's time to stop listening to that ego voice that tells you you're not good enough, smart enough, talented enough, capable enough, and whatever other "not enough's" there are. As I've said, it's just a conversation that you picked up when you were two or three or four or whenever. But it's not the truth about *who you are*.

There is a wonderful passage in *A Return to Love* by Marianne Williamson. It goes like this:

Our deepest fear is not that we are inadequate.
Our deepest fear is that we are powerful beyond measure.
It is our light, not our darkness, that most frightens us.
We ask ourselves, who am I to be brilliant, gorgeous,
talented and fabulous?
Actually, who are you *not* to be?
You are a child of God.
Your playing small doesn't serve the world.
There's nothing enlightened about shrinking so that
other people won't feel insecure around you.
We were born to make manifest the glory of God that is
within us.
It's not just in some of us; it's in everyone.
And as we let our own light shine, we unconsciously
give other people permission to do the same.

As we are liberated from our own fears,
our presence automatically liberates others.

Another equally moving sentiment comes from an Arthur Miller play. It goes like this:

> I dreamed I had a child, and even in the dream I saw it was my life, and it was an idiot, and I ran away. But it always crept into my lap again, clutched at my clothes. Until I thought, if I could kiss it, whatever in it was my own, perhaps I could sleep. And I bent to its broken face, and it was horrible... but I kissed it. I think one must finally take one's life in one's arms.

Take your life in your arms! Give up whatever conversation has you be "not enough." Take a stand for your greatness. You are brilliant, gorgeous, talented and fabulous. That's the truth. You were born to make manifest the glory of however you relate to the source of all life that has you be. As you let your own light shine and stop being critical of yourself, you begin to see the magnificence in others. You begin to create a space in your organization for everyone else to experience his or her own magnificence. It's truly a win/win game.

If this mindset change is a struggle for you, get a coach. There are many coaches today who work with people on this issue. We have many in our company that would be delighted and consider it a privilege to work with you. Or, you could find one on the Internet. Go to the web site of the International Coach Federation, www.coachfederation.org, and use its referral service to find the perfect coach for you.

Summary and Unshackled Leadership Action Items

When we were born, we arrived only with the voice of our higher consciousness, which told us that we were, like all others, whole, perfect and complete and a worthy and valuable human being. Unfortunately, it doesn't stay that way very long. The ego is born, with it's conversation that we are not good enough, not worthy and not loved or lovable. It's time to stop listening to the voice of the ego.

1. Create some quiet time, sit with a note pad and take an inventory of your life. You could do this with a trusted companion or preferably a coach or other trained professional. Write down the story of your life, focusing on the major events and the decisions you made about you as a result of those events.

2. Put those decisions into one of the three main conversations of the ego: I'm not good enough, I'm not worthy, or I'm not loved.

3. Then take each of the decisions and look for evidence that the contrary is the truth. In other words, challenge the early decisions you made and argue for a contrary conclusion. If you do this, I promise you'll find enormous evidence to refute the conversation of the ego.

4. Affirmations are a very powerful tool. An affirmation is a positive statement we tell ourselves over and over again until we learn to accept it as the truth. Create an affirmation for each of your limiting beliefs. Statements like: *I am a worthy and valuable human being.* Or: *I accept*

and love myself exactly the way I am and exactly the way I am not.

5. Start and end every day looking at yourself in a mirror and repeating your affirmations until you feel the truth of what you are saying. You can change your conversation, which will enable you to change your life!

To laugh often and much, to win the respect of intelligent people and the respect of children; to earn the appreciation of honest critics and endure the betrayal of false friends; to appreciate beauty, to find the best in others, to give of oneself; to leave the world a bit better, whether by a healthy child, a garden patch or a redeemed social condition, to have played and laughed with enthusiasm and sung with exultation; to know even one life has breathed easier; this is to have succeeded.

&. Ralph Waldo Emerson

Chapter 13

Complaints and Gossip

To survive in the existing paradigm, and to overcome our self deprecating beliefs, people develop various techniques and strategies that they use at work. We find these strategies at work in just about every company we encounter and the consequences are predictably deadly.

Two of the most common are 1) to complain and 2) to gossip. As used herein, a complaint is an expression of discontent with a person or a situation and gossip is making a derogatory statement to someone about a third person. Do you notice how often the people around you complain? Do you notice the ongoing complaints that *you* have? Before you continue, write down one or two of your favorite complaints to test the validity of the following discussion.

When we first start working with a company, one of the most debilitating realities we encounter is the amount and severity of the gossip. Many reasons exist for this, one of which we'll discuss here in conjunction with complaints. We'll discuss the other in Chapter 14.

In his treatise *The Passions, The Myth and Nature of Human Emotion* (University of Notre Dame Press, 1983) Robert C. Solomon says, "Every emotion is a strategy, a purposive attempt to structure our world in such a way as to maximize our sense of personal dignity and self-esteem. And, as strategies, our emotions can be more or less successful, more or less direct, well or ill conceived, effective or self-defeating... Every passion endows our lives with meaning, but every meaning is not ultimately meaningful, ultimately successful in maximizing our dignity and self-esteem and making possible the mutual respect and intimacy we desire."

In other words, Solomon says that everything a human being does when his self-esteem is in question and he's concerned with his survival is a strategy. These strategies can be either well or ill conceived. Survival strategies fall in the latter category.

Why do we do them? As Solomon says, "to maximize our sense of personal dignity and self-esteem." We want to feel okay in order to counter the underlying feeling of not okay. But strategies, while they do have this payoff, also have a big cost.

So people go around complaining and gossiping. Co-workers complain and gossip about each other, their supervisors, the company, everything. Management complains about the employees, the economy, the competition, the salespeople. It's a very popular game. Don't take responsibility; don't do anything about your complaint; don't take action; just settle for complaining and gossiping.

Here's another way of looking at what people get when they complain or gossip. First, they get to make somebody or something wrong, which, of course, makes them "right." They get to justify who they are and what they are doing, and they get to invalidate who the other person is and what he or she is doing. All of this makes them look good, again maximizing their sense of personal dignity and self-esteem.

The Vicious Cycle

The alternative to complaining is to confront the issue and take action. Indeed, some people do this some of the time. When they don't, the payoff is that they get to blame the other, avoid any responsibility in the matter, play safe and avoid risk by not confronting the other person.

So that's what we often do. We'll talk about the antidote later; but for now, recognize that a big survival game is likely going on in your company. Rather than taking responsibility, risking and getting into action, people settle for looking good, being right, justifying themselves and blaming others, all so they can feel good about themselves.

We pay a big price for this game. Remember the list of consequences for listening unconsciously with your attention on yourself and being concerned with your survival? The same list applies here. There is no communication, no understanding, no appreciation of the other person's position, no intimacy and certainly no trust. That costs you satisfaction, happiness, a sense of well being, self-confidence, joy, aliveness and ultimately the relationship. In a business setting, it costs productivity, creativity, teamwork, enthusiasm, turnover, success, and of course, money, results and accomplishment.

But there's more. When you complain and gossip instead of taking action, you turn yourself into a victim. After all, it's not *your* fault. "I can't do anything about it," you say, and that's the real definition of a victim. So you have two choices: 1) take responsibility or 2) be a victim. Once again, A or B. Many people choose the latter. I don't recommend it, and choice two certainly isn't the choice a leader in the new paradigm we're creating would make.

When you complain or gossip, you have no possibility of genuine satisfaction. You do get the brief satisfaction that comes from being right and making the other person wrong, but that's not genuine satisfaction.

When we do executive retreats, we take time for each participant to "tell one on himself" — to admit what he is complaining and/or gossiping about and what he is getting out of it. We then have people assess what it costs them to do that. We do this because people will only give up these survival games when they know what it's costing them. Otherwise, they have no reason to stop playing. People love to be right and look good...that is until they see what they give up for being right and looking good.

This is the time for people to get authentic. Complaints are an inauthentic way of being because complaining makes you look like you want something to happen, something to be different, even when you really don't. If you did want a different result, you'd take action. What you really want are the payoffs! It's about survival, about being right, about making other people wrong, about looking good, all to maximize your sense of personal dignity and self-esteem.

In every company where we've encountered it, gossip is a killer. It sucks the life out of everyone. People have the ability to be productive and creative, but not in the presence of gossip. When there's gossip, people's focus is on what's wrong and what's not working rather than on what's possible. Welcome to life and business in the twenty-first century!

Here's what's really sad. The results a company experiences are a direct function of who people are being, what their collective energy is focused on, the aliveness they bring to work, and their degree of alignment. Think back to our discussion of cause and effect and my definition of a successful organization: a group of enthusiastic, confident, optimistic, appreciative and happy people who work together on behalf of a future they have all committed themselves to. How can such a group prevail in an environment of gossip?

Every company has a mood. We don't pay a lot of attention to it, but we should pay more attention to it than anything else. Yes, there is an economy out there. Yes, there is competition. However, neither the economy nor the competition will ever do you in. Only you can do you in. If people focus their energy on making each other wrong, being right, being frustrated, being skeptical and being resigned rather than working together on behalf of an exciting future they have all committed themselves to, then it will be a long and tough road.

Where do we go from here? What's your job as a leader committed to the success of your enterprise? How do you remove the shackles and create the freedom to experience the extraordinary? It all depends on where you start. You have to *start* from being a group of enthusiastic, confident, optimistic, appreciative and happy people with faith and trust in you and the future, working together on behalf of a future you are all committed to. That, more than anything else, is your job. Get that accomplished and the rest will take care of itself.

Summary and Unshackled Leadership Action Items

Two of the most common survival strategies at work are 1) to complain and 2) to gossip. As used herein, a complaint is an expression of discontent with a person or a situation and gossip is making a derogatory statement to someone about a third person. Both are destructive and prevent an organization from moving forward powerfully and effectively.

1. Meet with your management team and take an inventory of what people are complaining about and what the office gossip is saying. Be sure it's safe for everyone to tell the truth because some of the gossip and complaints could be about you.
2. Develop an action plan to deal with every item on the list and get into action.
3. Figure out a way to communicate to every person in your organization that gossiping and complaining are no longer acceptable. Communicate to people in your organization that if they have a complaint, they need to communicate it openly and honestly and *only* to someone who can do something about it.
4. We would also highly recommend that you put teeth into this; that you communicate that gossiping and idle complaining is grounds for immediate termination. Many companies we've worked with have done this with very good results.
5. Of course, the flip side of this is the need to let people know that you authentically care about their complaints and are willing to do something about them so they communicate responsibly.

Chapter 14

The Dynamics of Our Relationships

Before we turn our attention to bringing this all together, let's discuss how everything we've learned so far plays out in our working relationships. We started this journey with the concept that we live in a particular paradigm. It isn't good and it isn't bad. It just is what it is. It has us be and act in a particular way. So *it*, not you or I, is responsible for our world being the way it is. The existing paradigm, the one right here and right now, is *not* set up to create a group of enthusiastic, confident, optimistic, appreciative and happy people who work together on behalf of a future they have all committed themselves to. On the contrary, it is set up to create pettiness, gossiping, competition, conflict, arguments and righteousness.

We live in a world where people think they are not okay. They have their attention on themselves, are concerned with their survival, are trying to make it and are coming from fear and scarcity. It's not a formula for success but it is the circumstances under which people wake up and go to work. As you can imagine, it produces the result it is designed for: pettiness, gossiping, competition, conflict, arguments and righteousness.

Let's explore how this impacts our relationships. Then we'll talk about how to clean up the mess that we make. Finally, we'll design a new paradigm for the twenty-first century and beyond. While the discussion about relationships will focus primarily on business relationships, everything said here applies to our personal relationships as well. Please read on with the broadest possible listening.

The First Encounter

All relationships start the same way. Someone comes to work in your company. You meet her and she meets you. The people already there meet her and vice versa. Often, not always, people experience an initial honeymoon stage. Everyone seems to be happy and it looks like things will work out. But what do we know about honeymoons? They are all too brief and eventually end!

This is predictable and inevitable because human beings are expectation-generating machines. We produce expectations so fast that if you could actually see it happening, it would make your head spin. It's the work of the ego and part of the "not okay" survival mechanism.

We have expectations about what the person will be like, what the relationship will be like, how the person will perform, how hard he'll work, and what his capabilities and talents are. Especially in a business context, human beings also have intentions. We intend something to happen, some result to be produced and some end product to be accomplished. We don't hire someone to do nothing. We intend for him to produce results.

It's not unusual in business for employers, employees, and co-workers to discuss some of these expectations and intentions. However, we seldom state *all* of our expectations and intentions and we generate new ones on a daily basis. The fact that this happens isn't bad or wrong; it just happens. It's entirely human.

The Letdown

Have you ever met anyone who fulfilled your expectations and lived up to your intentions all the time? While it would be wonderful if you could say yes, the answer is likely no. The only predictable result is that your expectations will be unfulfilled and your intentions will be thwarted. Whenever this occurs, you become disappointed.

Again, this is natural and to be expected. Since it's virtually impossible to stop having expectations, being disappointed is a part of life.

However, here's where we get into trouble. During workshops and speeches, I ask the attendees: "When you notice that you're disappointed, how many of you can honestly say that you *always* go over to the other person and communicate your disappointment to him or her?" A few hands may go up, but usually over 95% of the people admit they don't do that. At the very least, they admit that they don't do it all of the time.

Again, we have a number of seemingly valid reasons for this, all of which center around fear. Given that we are always concerned with our survival, communicating something distasteful threatens our survival. If the disappointment is with a supervisor, manager or executive, we fear that communicating threatens our job, our income or our relationship with that person.

Since nobody ever taught us *how* to communicate, we don't know how to speak without judgment. Our past experiences with communicating disappointments are usually negative, so we don't want to rock the boat. We assume our communication will trigger an upset. People often tell us they don't want to hurt the other person's feelings. However, our belief is that the person doesn't want to deal with the upset that they expect will occur.

The biggest reason people don't communicate, as discussed in Chapter 4, is that people do not know how to listen. You can almost count on people to get defensive and to take your communication personally. Maybe they'll wait patiently until you are finished, maybe not. Either way, we expect them to launch into a defense and counterattack. It seems better not to say anything and stuff it. But is it?

Instead of communicating, we go into what we call the metaphorical file room in our mind. This file room is an amazing place. No matter how much is stored in the file room, there's always room for more. No matter how many files are already there, there is a seemingly endless collection of empty file folders. Got the picture?

So the first time this new person disappoints you, you open the file room, find an empty file folder, put the person's name on the folder, and deposit the undelivered communication (the disappointment, the unfulfilled expectation, the thwarted intention) into the file folder. We then file it away for the time being. When the next disappointment occurs, or the same one repeats itself, we make another entry in the file...and then another and another.

The Result

During the honeymoon period, everything is wonderful because you're not dealing with a lot of disappointments. You can be open and intimate with the other person and you usually have a high degree of trust. On the scale of openness, intimacy and trust, you could say that 100% is available to you.

But every entry you put in the "file" displaces the possibility of 100% openness, intimacy and trust. Think of it like a glass of water that's filled to the brim where the water represents openness, intimacy and trust. If you start pouring sand into the glass, where the sand represents the undelivered communications, it's evident that the water will start spilling out.

So one day you have 100% openness, intimacy and trust, and you feel wonderful about the other person. Before you know it, you're down to 90%. Ninety percent isn't all that bad, but it doesn't feel quite as good as 100%. You're not quite as eager to be open with the other person, but it's not too bad.

However, the sand keeps going into the glass, the disappointments keep going into the file, and now you're down to 80% on the scale of openness, intimacy and trust. You're starting to suffer a bit. It's getting harder and harder to be with the other person and to talk openly and honestly. You start avoiding, maybe being a bit sarcastic, but you continue on.

You can see where this is going. Eventually you get to the point where you will not put up with it any further. During this process, your ego plays a very interesting game with you.

When this process of making entries into the file first started, at some level you knew you contributed something to your upset and you knew you should have communicated your feelings to the other person. However, you didn't and you still don't because of all the reasons we've discussed. As the "file" gets bigger and bigger you lose all sense of your responsibility and you become convinced that the source of your increasing upset is the other person. "If he would just... (fill in the blank)." This is when your ego starts having its way with you.

The Mood Shifts

At this point, one of several things happens. In personal relationships, people fight and argue and perhaps split up or get divorced. I'm convinced that these withheld communications are the primary reason why most personal relationships turn sour or end. In business, people complain and gossip or they leave.

Have you ever been in a situation where you said or did something and another person reacted in a way that was dramatically disproportionate to what you said or did? Of course! Have you ever been in a situation where somebody else said or did something and you reacted in a way that was dramatically disproportionate to what the other person said or did? Of course you did that too.

We call that "file emptying time." You (or the other person) don't react just to what was said or done at that moment; you or they react with all the fury that exists in the accumulated file. Given that the reaction is totally out of proportion to what just happened, the recipient of the file dumping is caught off guard and is bewildered, almost guaranteeing that he or she will take the communication personally, get defensive and attack back. It's an ugly situation and one we have all had an opportunity to experience.

Sometimes, instead of the file emptying, the other person is turned into the enemy. You drift apart and fight about something, everything. The file becomes evidence of something negative about the other person and you start to use the file against him and make him wrong. It's another version of the survival game. And, of course, the payoff is that you get to be right.

We've gone into organizations and experienced these occurrences in many forms. Sometimes people learn to be polite with each other, but you can feel the underlying tension. Everybody knows it's there, but nobody is willing to confront it. People become like strangers in the night, exchanging pleasantries and doing the best they can to make the most of a bad situation and get on with what they have to do. Definitely not a formula for a championship team.

Sometimes it's worse. We've gone into organizations where it seems that people come to work, climb into their foxholes, arm themselves, and dare anyone to walk into their space. It can get ugly.

How it All Unfolds

In 2001, I gave a speech to a group of people in the office building and management business. After the speech, the president of a real estate development company that had four operating divisions took me aside to talk to me. The divisions, development, construction, property management, and leasing, as well as a finance department, each had one or more executives in charge. Nine people, including the president, human resources manager and information services manager were on the management team.

During the conversation, I asked the president how the relationships between the executives were. His answer was that they were awful (he used a different word, but I want to keep it clean). I went to the company's headquarters and interviewed all nine executives. As usual, I heard lots of judgments, withheld communications and disappointments. The woman who headed up development was very aggressive, which you want in that position. However, she did a lot of things that people didn't understand. She never bothered to explain her reasons and they never bothered to ask. As a result, nobody trusted her.

The people in construction were convinced that the people in finance did everything they could possibly do to make their lives miserable and, of course, the people in finance couldn't understand why the people in construction were so difficult to deal with. The gentleman in leasing had insecurities about how the president felt regarding his performance, was convinced he was disappointing the president, but never bothered to verify any of his assumptions. The president didn't have a clue how to handle any of this and hoped it would somehow handle itself.

What happened here, and what happens all the time, is that people generate a conversation — a listening about the other people — and that becomes who they are for them. It's no longer a judgment or opinion; they *are* that way. Our listening becomes the space in which they get to show up. They just keep showing up that way, and we get to be right once again.

The Reality of Life Revealed

We've gone as deeply into the existing paradigm as is necessary to understand why most, if not nearly all organizations, don't fit my definition of a successful organization; that is, a group of enthusiastic, confident, optimistic, appreciative and happy people who work together on behalf of a future they have all committed themselves to. When you grow up in a world where you learn to believe that you are not okay, where you have your attention on yourself, where you are concerned with your own survival, where your conversation is dominated by the ego, when you come from fear and scarcity, when you look for satisfaction and happiness in the circumstances of life, when you listen right/wrong, get to the point, when you use language to talk about what you think is there rather than using it to create what's there, when you withhold your communications and complain, gossip and build files, you certainly don't have a formula for success, happiness and joy. That's the world we inherited, and that's the reality. It doesn't pay to fight it. It makes a lot more sense to understand it, acknowledge it and get to work putting in the antidote. That is what the remaining chapters will discuss.

Summary and Unshackled Leadership Action Items

While there is usually a short honeymoon stage at the beginning of all relationships, both personally and professionally, it doesn't usually last very long because it doesn't take long before the disappointments start mounting up. Instead of communicating our disappointments, we "file them away" and the accumulating file becomes evidence of the unsatisfactory nature of the relationship.

1. We will discuss in the next chapter how to deal with this. In the meantime, take an inventory of the people in your life, both personally and at work, and make a list of everyone that you have disappointments about and who you can see you have something to say to that you are not saying.
2. Make a similar list of people in your life, both personally and professionally, who you believe have things to say to you that they are likely not saying.
3. With regard to each of the people on your lists, take a look at what it's costing you to have them on your lists or to likely be on their list. Are you experiencing openness, intimacy, joy, appreciation and trust in your relationships? If not, it may be time to empty some files. That's what the next chapter is about.

Chapter 15

Cleaning up the Mess

Before we move forward to design a new paradigm, you may need to first "clean up the mess" that you or others in your company have made as a result of being with each other in the way discussed in Chapter 14. In almost every company we've worked with, unspoken upsets and disappointments exist, meaning we are not dealing with a clean slate. To create a mutually satisfying future on top of the unspoken upsets would be like trying to build a skyscraper over a swamp. The unresolved upsets will weaken the foundation of the new paradigm, making a meaningful and satisfying result impossible.

The number one requirement for cleaning up the messes people make in their relationships is that they have to be willing to go back in time and "clean out the trash." They must be willing to let go of the unfulfilled expectations, the thwarted intentions and the resulting upsets and disappointments — not to get even or dump — but to let go.

In our experience, people need to be not only willing, but also anxious to clean up the mess they've made in their relationships

173

with each other so they can restore intimacy, openness and trust and get their relationships back.

Usually people are willing and anxious, but occasionally a few have such a vested interest in being right and in winning that even the offer of peace and harmony is not appealing. You might run into people like this yourself.

Moving Ahead

I remember the first time we did a retreat based on the approach this book teaches. It was for a group of partners of a law firm in Texas. Two firms with very different cultures had merged. The clashes were predictable and regular. They had hired three different consultants over a three-year period but each failed to bridge the gap between the two groups. The firm's administrator called to see if we could help.

I did the retreat with one of my associates at the time, a gentleman named Craig. We took the fifteen partners to the same hotel they had used four years in a row. We began by talking with them, asking questions and getting feedback. After several hours, we said to them: "We are now going to take a break. For the last few hours we've been courting you, inviting you into a game that will heal your relationships with each other and leave you in action, working together on behalf of a future you can all be committed to. It's now time to get the work done. If, after everything we've said, you don't feel like you want to participate, you should honor your integrity, tell us you are not willing to participate and leave."

As soon as we started the break, one of the partners told us he was leaving. When we asked him why, he said that it all sounded like a bunch of BS to him, that most of his partners were assholes, and that he didn't think this would do any good. He left. He was so committed to being right that he was not willing to give the process a try. He couldn't see the forest for the trees.

The good news is that people like him are rare. Most people are cautious but willing to move ahead. Let's learn what moving ahead looks like.

Towards a Partnership Paradigm

My intention is for you to use the information presented thus far to enable you and others in your company to learn how to talk to each other, how to speak and listen, and how to responsibly communicate unfulfilled expectations, thwarted intentions and disappointments so you and they can empty the files and return to where your relationships started, a place of openness, intimacy and trust. Under those circumstances, you can begin to design a new paradigm for being that will allow for true teamwork and what we call "partnership."

The "file emptying" is a multi-stage process.

Stage One: Take an Inventory

The first stage is to write down what's in the file. Here are the statements I recommend you use:

- My expectations of you that are unfulfilled are...
- My intentions for you/us that have been thwarted are...
- I am disappointed with you/our relationship in that...

- What I'm not saying to you is… (or What I'd like to say
  to you is …)
- What I'd like to acknowledge you for is…

Before I tell you what this accomplishes, try it for yourself. Pick someone in your company who you have things to say to — unfulfilled expectations, thwarted intentions and/or disappointments — and take some time to write down your answers to the above statements. You will find the exercise quite revealing.

❧

This stage serves several purposes. First, you are writing about yourself. Remember, when you're upset with someone, your ego convinces you that the source of the upset is the other person. These statements force you to look at the upset from the perspective of responsibility, which is a fundamental intention of this whole exercise. Once people begin to see that the real source of their upset is *their* unfulfilled expectations and *their* thwarted intentions, the desire to blame the other person begins to dissipate.

Second, when a person is upset, the upset seems like a huge mass of things that are wrong with the other person. The mind is not a useful place to store and sort out upsets. It's the home of the ego where only mischief can occur. By getting your thoughts down on paper, you begin to notice there wasn't as much to the "file" as you thought and you see that your upsets and disappointments stem from a few, manageable issues.

Third, people consistently report they already start feeling better once they get their feelings on paper. Getting the disappointments out of their head begins to dissipate the energy that the upset contains.

Stage Two: Communicate

How to speak: If you were going to communicate everything in your "file" to another person, how would you manage your communication? It's evident that being accusatory, yelling, finger pointing and attacking would be non-productive (even though that's exactly what we often do). Instead, speak to the other person with respect and compassion. After all, there is another human being on the other side of your communication.

Remain calm, be open and honest, and say exactly what you need to say without sugar coating it. Listeners find it annoying if they feel the speaker is trying to protect their feelings by being "nice."

At the same time, it's critical that you not be righteous but rather communicate from a place of responsibility. If you become righteous, the listener will feel like you are "wronging" him. He will want to justify and defend himself, all of which will defeat the purpose of the exercise.

At this point many people ask, "Why would I want to say it all, especially the things I don't want to confront?" I hope the answer is obvious. You need to completely empty the file, for it's only when the file is completely empty that there can be 100% openness, intimacy and trust. If you leave anything in the file, it becomes like a cancer that will grow and eventually cause another upset.

Some of the things we learned as children keep us stuck in the existing paradigm. One of these childhood messages is that if you don't have something good to say, you shouldn't say anything. If we took this instruction literally, we would never communicate our upsets and disappointments, and our inevitable files would grow and grow. Obviously, that old childhood message is not very useful.

How to Listen: If someone were going to tell you everything in her file, how would you listen? From our discussion thus far, you know how *not* to listen. The way to listen is to *"just get it!"* Listen with compassion. Get your attention off yourself, get over there with the other person and get how it is for her. Recreate what it must be like for the speaker.

Encourage the other person to say everything, and say nothing in response other than "thank you" or "I'm sorry" or both. Do not react, do not listen as if you're being made wrong and don't take anything the other person says personally, even though it is personal.

You might think this is a set-up for something painful. After all, you're going to sit and listen while somebody says all kinds of things about you, and all you get to do is thank them, perhaps say you're sorry, and encourage them to say more.

Rest assured that there is a good reason for being willing to listen in this way. First, people have the experience of being heard, which is enormously satisfying and fulfilling. Second, it allows the speaker to empty his file. What's in it for you is the rehabilitation of the relationship, which is something both parties want.

Equally important, you'll learn things about yourself, the other person, and what's going on in your company that will amaze or surprise you.

We did this work with a client company in Florida. When we told the COO that we would give his managers an opportunity to communicate everything in their files to him and his job was to "just get it" and say thank you, he thought it would be difficult. Reluctantly he agreed to try it.

When we spoke to him after the event, his reaction was typical. He said that while he heard some things he expected, he was truly amazed at some of the feedback people gave him. He had no idea that some of the things that had happened at the company had impacted his managers in the ways they did. Some people said things that were completely opposite of what he thought. While I guarantee you it wasn't easy for him to listen to some of the things said, he was profoundly appreciative of going through the experience.

When we do this in a retreat environment, we have each person take a turn sitting in a chair in the middle of the room. Everyone then tells the person what they have been "filing." The speakers use the five statements from step one as a guide and the listener gets to listen. He doesn't respond; he just gets the other persons' communication.

You may be asking, "Isn't this embarrassing, a horrible experience, to ask someone to sit in front of all of his peers and have them communicate their unfulfilled expectations, their thwarted intentions and their disappointments? Wouldn't it be better to do this one-on-one in private?" No, and for several reasons.

First, if you want to build a sense of team, you need to end the "private" communications. Everybody knows what's going on anyway, so it's time to stop pretending to keep this all a "secret."

Second, if John were to communicate to Fred privately, it would be very easy for Fred to ignore what John says and deflect the value in the communication, thinking it's only John's issue. But if Fred is sitting in a room with all his team members, and several people (or everyone) communicate the same thing to him, it's hard to ignore the comments.

People always say or do things that upset others. Most of the time, we don't know what they are or what the impact is because nobody tells us. When you're sitting in a room, surrounded by your team members, with all of them communicating their unfulfilled expectations, thwarted intentions and disappointments, it's impossible to not have the feedback sink in.

With the fifteen Texas law firm partners I discussed earlier, it took half of the first day and most of the second day to complete step two. Each partner had the opportunity to communicate all the disappointments that had developed over the years since the merger, all of the unfulfilled expectations about how they would work together and all of the thwarted intentions in the results that didn't get produced.

During this process, the hurtful energy in the room dissipated as the upsets were communicated and released. And in the process, people were learning to take responsibility for their upsets and disappointments, to communicate responsibly and to listen with compassion.

When we started day three of this retreat, we went around the room and asked if anybody had anything to share before we continued. One of the partners responded that his wife had called him earlier that morning to ask how it was going. He related that he told his wife he had witnessed a miracle and if he hadn't witnessed what he had seen with his own eyes he wouldn't have believed it. Everyone else in the room said they felt the same way. Rather than being a horrible experience, it liberated them. That continues to be the reaction from the now thousands of people who have gone through the same process.

In another firm we worked with, over forty people attended the retreat. Given the impracticality of having everyone communicate with each person individually, we had each participant come to the front of the room and say whatever he or she wasn't saying to the group in general and/or to someone in particular.

The first day of this retreat was fairly uneventful, with no major revelations or disappointments. The morning of the second day, however, one of the participants got up in front of the group and, in great detail and with a great amount of emotion, spoke about his ten years as a practicing alcoholic, all of which time he was a member of this firm. He hadn't had a drink for eight years and regularly went to AA meetings, but it was a big secret he lived with. In AA, one of the twelve steps is to make amends, but he didn't know how to do that with such a large group of partners. This became his opportunity.

I stood at the side of the room and listened with compassion, which was the instruction given to everyone else. As he emptied his file, I was so moved by his open and honest sharing that tears started to stream down my face. I reached for my handkerchief. That's when I noticed that virtually everyone in the room was also reaching for a tissue (we always have boxes of tissues at these events). When he finished, there wasn't a dry eye in the house. Everyone leaped to their feet and gave him a standing ovation. It was an extraordinary experience none of us who were there will ever forget. More important, the process of bonding and building a sense of team among this group had begun.

As soon as he sat down, a hand in the back of the room shot up. So I asked, "Oh, are you next?" He said, "Absolutely. If I don't do this now, I'll never do it." So this next partner comes up to the front of the room, turns to his partners and says, "What I'm not saying to you is that I'm gay." He then proceeded to say more about his sexual preference and his gay relationships.

When he was done, one of the other partners stood up and asked, "Are you crazy? We know you're gay; we've always known you're gay. You're not our gay partner John; you're our partner John."

John stood there in disbelief. He had been with this firm for twenty-eight years and all that time he lived with this secret. However, the only one who thought it was a secret was him! At the end of the day, when we went around the room and gave everyone a chance to say what they wanted to say to be complete for the day, John stood up and said, "This is the happiest day of my whole life!"

That's what our current paradigm is costing people — not having the freedom to communicate, not having any real listening, and not having the opportunity to be heard. I'd venture to say that's what's likely going on with the people in your company and in your life, with your co-workers, your employees, your family and your friends. It's not because you're bad or wrong; rather, it's because you're a human being. Now you can change all of that.

Stage Three: Apologize

The third stage is to apologize. Unfortunately, most people do not understand and appreciate the power of an apology.

People frequently think that the phrase "I apologize" means "I'm sorry." It doesn't. While people in our culture often use the two terms interchangeably, we think you shouldn't do that. The word "sorry" is derived from the word "sorrow." In essence, when you say, "I'm sorry," you're saying "I feel sad" or "I experience sorrow over that." "I'm sorry" is an expression of your feelings. That's why, when people are sitting in the center and others are communicating to them, we let them say "I'm sorry" if someone says something that generates sadness in them.

"I apologize," on the other hand, is entirely different. "I apologize" includes three distinct elements. First, it's an acknowledgement. I acknowledge what you said; I acknowledge what I did or didn't do; I acknowledge what I said or didn't say; I acknowledge the substance of your communication.

Second, it's a willingness to take responsibility. Third, it's a request for forgiveness.

How This Works: After the Texas law firm retreat, the partners decided to let all their employees empty their files to the partners. Because there were many employees, we divided them into groups of thirty and spent the morning training them in this speaking and listening approach. After lunch, we had the partners sit in front of the room. Each employee had an opportunity to say what he or she was not saying. Excited about doing this at your company?

One secretary turned to one of the partners and said: "Paul, what I'm not saying to you is that when I pass you in the hall in the morning, I say 'good morning' but you don't respond. So when you are gone, I turn to the wall and say 'good morning' to the wall. I want you to know I get more satisfaction saying 'good morning' to the wall than I get saying 'good morning' to you because I don't expect a response from the wall!"

Her words were an embarrassment and a blow to Paul. But Paul wasn't a bad guy. Actually, he was a good guy. Like many of us, though, he was so focused on himself and what he had to do that he was often oblivious to what was going on around him. Her words were a huge wake up call. Because he was so unaware of this, he was profoundly appreciative of this secretary saying what she said.

All Paul could do was apologize. He couldn't go back and change what had happened. He could only clean up the consequences and hurt feelings about what happened and move forward from there.

He apologized by saying, "I apologize for not paying attention to you, for not being appreciative of your desire to be friendly, for not responding to you, and for appearing like an insensitive, uncaring, unappreciative jerk." (The last word wasn't necessary, but it helped her have the experience of being heard.) He acknowledged what she said, acknowledged what he did or didn't do, took responsibility, and while not stated, he invited her to forgive him. She did.

People are often reluctant to apologize because they feel an apology is an admission of wrong or guilt. They think that by apologizing, they are saying, "I was bad. I was wrong. You were right." Since human beings always want to be right and look good, that's a significant barrier to apologizing.

One of the most valuable lessons you can learn from this book is that the above perception is not what an apology means. Not at all. An apology is truly a gift that you give to the other person. It doesn't make you look weak at all. Just the opposite. It allows others to have that wonderful experience of being heard, which they much appreciate. Rather than appearing weak, you show up as their hero.

My friend and mentor Lew Epstein was fond of saying that when you were born, you were given an infinite supply of apologies so make sure you use them up before you die.

I once worked with seven partners of a firm who had grown up with each other. They all met when they were teenagers living in a drug rehabilitation facility. As they freed themselves from their addictions, they worked together in the facility. When their work at the facility came to an end, they decided to take their experience and enter the business world as partners in a commercial enterprise.

As you can imagine, because they had been together for so long, they had quite a few things stuffed in their files. In our first retreat, they cleared the air and revealed all that they had been holding in. The amazing part was when we came to the apologies. They apologized to each other for over two hours. They were so committed to making sure everyone had the experience of being heard that they were unwilling to leave out anything. They apologized sincerely for all the things they could each see they did that was in any way hurtful to any of the others. They finally emptied their files.

Stage Four: Forgiveness

Stage four of the file-emptying process is forgiveness. The definition I use of forgiveness is:

To give up resentment against or the desire to punish; to stop being angry with; to pardon. To give up the claim to punish or exact penalty for (an offense); to overlook. To give as before.

The last sentence captures what forgiveness is about. The actual word "forgiveness" comes from the expression "to give as before." It means that you return yourself to the place you were before the transgression you are forgiving someone for happened. You wipe the slate clean, start all over and let go.

Because of the influence of the ego, most people are not very good at forgiving. The ego wants us to be right; to not take responsibility; and we like to blame, look good, justify ourselves and invalidate others. For those and many other reasons, when somebody does something that offends us, we automatically assume he is at fault and we are justified in our anger and upset. However, that's not a formula for peace or happiness. Not forgiving is like picking up a handful of hot coals to throw at another person, or taking poison and waiting for the other person to die.

In other words, when we don't forgive, we are the ones who suffer. We think we are happy because we are right, but we aren't happy. We are the ones carrying around the anger and hurt. The majority of the time the other person doesn't have a clue that we are angry and upset so she certainly doesn't suffer.

There's more. A major article in the October 23, 2003 issue of *USA Today* has the headline: "Forgiveness could be balm for the body, too." Some of the things the article says are: "Overall, findings show a link between forgiveness and health, says Everett Worthington, executive director of the group (A Campaign for Forgiveness Research, a non-profit organization that promotes studies). 'Chronic unforgiveness causes stress,' he says. 'Every time people think of their transgressor, their body responds.'

"Blood pressure and heart rates go up. Facial muscles tense, stress hormones kick in. Chronic stress affects the immune and cardiovascular systems, he says. Forgiveness reduces stress by replacing 'negative emotions with positive ones.'"

During retreats, or whenever we facilitate a file emptying between individuals or groups of individuals, we ask the individuals if they are willing to forgive each other. We make it clear that there are three choices. "Yes," "No," and "I'm committed to it, but not prepared to do it yet; I'll work on it and keep you posted."

I always put in the third alternative so people can choose with authenticity. Sometimes it's not so simple to forgive. In my own life, one of my daughters carried a lot of hurt from her childhood about who I was for her during those early years. We sat many times and talked about it. She would empty her file and cry, and I would apologize, but her hurt wouldn't go away. She would periodically leave, heal, get some help and come back and try to forgive again. It has taken her many years to get to the bottom of it and finally forgive. The process still continues to this day.

Friends of mine, a married couple, had a similar ordeal. At one point in the marriage, the wife chose to have an affair with another man. She quickly learned that an affair was not what she wanted. The affair actually strengthened her commitment to the marriage, so she ended it. However, she was clear she could not live with the consequences of keeping the affair a secret from her husband. She felt that the risk of telling him was clearly less than the risk of keeping it a secret.

So she told him. The details of what happened are not that relevant. He said what he said and she said what she said. She apologized and expressed her commitment to the relationship. However, he could not easily forgive her. She said that the next year was like living in hell. However, he was committed to forgiving her and over time he did.

Similar situations exist in business. Fortunately, in over 98% of the cases, people are smart enough to realize that if they don't forgive, the only one they hurt is them self and so they forgive. There are occasional occurrences where people opt for choice three: they are committed to forgiving and say that they will work on it. There are rare occurrences where people won't forgive which, by the way, isn't so bad. If you discover there is someone in your organization who would rather be right than forgive, that is very useful information, as they just might not be the kind of person you want in your company.

Remember the lawyer who left the retreat in Texas? At the end of the retreat, the partners who stayed were so thrilled with the result that they decided to do the retreat again and include some people who couldn't make the first one. When they invited the lawyer who left to participate, he refused. So they invited him to leave the firm, which he did. The ones who remained were much better off because they didn't have to deal with his ever-present anger.

Stage Five: Acknowledgment

Now we're ready to complete the process, and that's what stage five is for. If I were a minister and what I just described to you were a wedding ceremony, I would pronounce you man and wife and say you can now kiss the bride. But I'm not a minister, and this is not a wedding ceremony; it is another kind of ceremony. While I don't know what you will feel is appropriate to do, I do know that at the appropriate time you'll look into your heart and know what you need to do.

In my experience, people always know what to do. Depending on the level of intimacy that exists in the group, several things happen. Men, especially those who have a hard time being intimate, shake hands and sometimes exchange a brief hug. For other people, the hugs are more meaningful. I've seen many people hug each other for extended periods. I've also seen a fair amount of tears shed as people express their appreciation for what they have just been through and their sadness and regret for not doing it sooner. In any event, the files are emptied, the air is clean and fresh and people are ready for a new beginning.

Summary and Unshackled Leadership Action Items

Emptying the files you have with others and allowing them to empty their files with you is a multi-stage process:

- Take an inventory by writing down what's in the "file."
- Communicate and listen appropriately
- Apologize
- Forgive
- Acknowledge each other

1. With regard to those people in your life and your company with whom you feel confident that you can do

this without the meeting turning into a confrontation, go ahead and meet with them, explain the process and do the file emptying.

2. With regard to those people with whom you are not so confident a confrontation won't result, get a neutral third party to facilitate the file emptying.

3. If you can see that this is a significant issue in your company, you might want to seriously consider having us or someone else conduct a retreat for you and your team to clean up the mess and restore you to a place of openness, intimacy and trust.

4. Start with people for whom there is not a lot at stake so you can get comfortable with the process. As you see how it works, you can get into more and more uncomfortable situations.

5. Remember, the key to making this work is your willingness to make it safe for others to communicate to you. You do this by just getting their communication, listening with compassion, not getting defensive and not arguing with what they have to say.

Chapter 16

A New Beginning

Where do we go from here? I hope that the answers to that question are already apparent. You can now understand why John Stuart Mill said, "When society requires to be rebuilt, there is no use in attempting to rebuild it on the old plan. No great improvements in the lot of mankind are possible, until a great change takes place in the fundamental constitution of their modes of thought."

I trust you can now understand the basic premise of this book: that we live in a particular paradigm which is neither good nor bad. It just is what it is. It makes us be and act in a particular way. So *it*, not you or I or the people in your company are responsible for our world being the way it is. The existing paradigm, the one right here and right now, is *not* set up to have a group of enthusiastic, confident, optimistic, appreciative and happy people who work together on behalf of a future they have all committed themselves to. To the contrary, it is set up to have pettiness, gossiping, competition, conflict, arguments, and righteousness. Why is it this way?

As I explained earlier, we have a split mind. The upper mind is the home of our "higher consciousness." This is the voice of peace, love, oneness, togetherness, and harmony. Theologians call this the voice of God. Call it whatever you want.

The lower mind is the home of the ego. It is the part of our mind that was programmed the way I showed in my description of the birth of "the conversation." As we will see, it is the voice of fear, limitation, separation, scarcity, and greed.

I trust that you appreciate that the ego is not your friend. It doesn't have your best interests at heart. For the vast majority of people, the ego always speaks loudest and always speaks first. The voice of the ego is often so loud we never hear the voice of our higher consciousness. Even when we are called into action by that voice, the ego all too frequently fights it tooth and nail.

As I said before, I believe life is not all that complicated. In fact, at least in theory, it's simple. Always two choices, A or B. Listen to the voice of the ego or listen to the voice of your higher consciousness.

If we keep operating in the existing paradigm, listening to the voice of the ego, we'll only get more of what we've got. It's necessary that we be clear about the existing paradigm and see it for what it is and how it has us be as human beings. Our discussion thus far has made it apparent why our companies, indeed our world, are in the shape they are in.

Here's the wonderful and liberating reality: the way we are as human beings, dominated by the ego, is only one possible way of being a human being. We are proposing an alternate paradigm, a paradigm designed to create cooperation, caring, cohesiveness, trust, respect, and most important, satisfaction, fulfillment, harmony, creativity and productivity.

Once we commit to this alternate way of being, our lives begin to flow smoothly. Set up the field in the shape of a diamond, add bases and a pitcher's mound, and it's easy to play baseball. All you need to do is practice the new way of being until you get good at it, an exciting and enlivening experience if you're willing to commit yourself to it. See my point? A or B!

The Importance of Commitment

As you move forward, take the critical step of finding out who is on your team and who isn't. In personal relationships as well as in business, people often wait to see the result before they commit. They say, "I'll try out this relationship, this job, whatever, and see how it goes. If it works out, or at least looks like it will work out, then I'll commit."

Unfortunately, this way of being almost guarantees that it's *not* going to work out. What makes relationships work out is being committed to them working out. Remember the law of cause and effect. If you're waiting to see how it turns out, you produce more waiting to see how it turns out.

If you want it to turn out, commit! Remember our definition of a successful enterprise? It's a group of people working together on behalf of a future they have all *committed themselves to!* Does this guarantee things will work out? Unfortunately no, because there are a lot of other factors to consider. However, it does stack the odds in your favor.

At the end of our retreats, we ask each person, "Are you willing to commit yourself to working with this group of people to design and create a future that you are all aligned with? No holding back; no waiting any more to see how it turns out? Are you willing to close the back door, put both feet in instead of one foot out and one foot in, and be willing to do whatever it takes to produce the result you all align on?"

You might think that's a lot to ask of anyone. What's remarkable is that in the space created by emptied files, people almost always enthusiastically say yes. With that yes, they open the door to an enormous new possibility.

Stand Taking

Before we complete the discussion of the new paradigm, we have one more topic to discuss.

In the ordinary course of events, we are constantly making decisions about one thing or another. You could say that your job, more than anything else, is to make decisions. That's both good news and bad news about being a leader. It's good because you are the one who ultimately gets to make the decisions. It's bad because the process is often challenging and difficult, fraught with uncertainty.

So let's look at the decision-making process. Where do you normally look or what do you check in with when you have to make a decision? As with all the ideas we've discussed in this book, don't look for "the answer;" inquire into this.

Let me suggest one possibility. It's not the "truth;" it's just something to consider. Consider that you first determine what you think about the situation you are dealing with, and then you determine how you feel about the situation. Assuming for the moment that this is true, where do these thoughts and feelings come from? I suggest they come from your experiences to date.

When in time did those experiences occur? In the past. When we look to our thoughts and feelings in our decision-making process, the future often resembles some version of the past.

This explains why so many people never change the events in their lives. They keep doing the same thing over and over again because they keep living their lives out of the thoughts and feelings they've created in the past.

The question is: "Is there another way?" Is there something you and I have access to so that we can create a future that, while honoring the past, is not an extension of the past? Absolutely!

We have a mouth and we have the ability to open that mouth and speak into existence a future that is not otherwise going to occur. That's called *taking a stand!*

As Max Weber, the German philosopher once said:

I am under the impression that in nine out of ten cases I deal with windbags who do not fully realize what they take upon themselves, but who intoxicate themselves with romantic sensations. From a human point of view this is not very interesting to me, nor does it move me profoundly. However, it is immensely moving when a mature man — no matter whether old or young in years — is aware of a responsibility for the consequences of his conduct and really feels such a responsibility with heart and soul. He then acts by following the ethic of responsibility and somewhere he reaches the point where he says: 'Here I stand; I can do no other.' That is something genuinely human and moving. And every one of us who is not spiritually dead must realize the possibility of finding himself at some time in that position.

History abounds with examples of the course of human events being changed because a person or a group followed the ethic of responsibility, as Max Weber defined it, and took a stand for some new course of action or possibility. The United States of America was created when our forefathers got together, took a stand and declared their independence. Mahatma Gandhi changed the course of history when he took a stand for a free India. Martin Luther King, Jr. changed the awareness of people in the United States and launched the civil rights movement with his famous speech on the steps of the Lincoln Memorial. President John F. Kennedy launched the race to the moon when he took a stand for the possibility of landing a man on the moon and returning him safely.

Stand taking has tremendous power. As a leader in the new paradigm you will always have to make decisions. The question in the future will be: "Where will you look to find your answers?" Will you look to your thoughts and feelings, or will you look someplace else, such as to your commitments, your vision, your mission, your intentions or your goals? We'll look further at this as we discuss designing the future of your company.

For now, I want to point out what may already be obvious. Taking a stand is risky business. Look at what happened to President Lincoln, Gandhi, Martin Luther King, Jr. and our forefathers. The first three got killed and our forefathers had a war on their hands.

While taking a stand is risky business, it's what distinguishes the ordinary leader from the extraordinary leader. Being willing to take stands is what ultimately will make you powerful and effective.

Summary and Unshackled Leadership Action Items

We live in a paradigm which is *not* set up to have a group of enthusiastic, confident, optimistic, appreciative and happy people who work together on behalf of a future they have all committed themselves to. To the contrary, it is set up to have pettiness, gossiping, competition, conflict, arguments and righteousness. In order to move beyond the constraints of the existing paradigm, you'll need to do two things:

- Commit yourself to a new possibility
- Take a stand for what you truly believe and the future you are going to create.

1. As an unshackled leader, you must get clear about what you're committed to. Given what you've learned so far out of reading this book, what are the fundamental commitments that you will stand for as you lead your company into the future?
2. Meet with your management team, share your commitments with them and see who is willing to join you in these commitments. Of course, this action must be preceded by a "file emptying" as explained in the previous chapter.

Why are we here? To create partnership. As fellow travelers on a common voyage, our purpose is clear. We can celebrate the opportunity to reclaim a quality of relationship that is the birthright of all people... Thank you for your courage, and bless you on your journey towards partnership in relationship.
❧ Lew Epstein

Chapter 17

A New Paradigm of Being Human

In the previous chapters, I've painted what looks like a bleak picture of the current paradigm and the typical conversation in which we live. If you look below the surface, you'll see how true this picture is. Why? By now the answer should be obvious. Our conversation is dominated by the ego. Like one of the wolves in the Cherokee tale, it's a pretty ugly conversation.

Fortunately, another way of being human exists, a way that doesn't come with such a high price tag. In fact, this alternative paradigm of being human encourages and supports people to become unshackled leaders who empower others and make the organization they lead one worth being a part of. It's only this way of being that will give you the freedom to experience the extraordinary.

In designing our new way of being, the most obvious question is: "What's this human being's conversation going to be in regards to him or herself?" The new conversation is "I'm okay!" Why? Because being willing to take a stand for the most fundamental thing you can stand for — your own worth and value — is a critical step. As discussed in Chapter 12, as long as you're critical of yourself you'll be critical of others. That's just the way it is. To reach your full potential as a leader you must first commit to resolving the issues you have with you! Start with taking responsibility for the conversation you have about you, eliminating the "not okay" conversation, and generating a conversation that you are, indeed, okay!

The second question regarding our alternative paradigm is: "What's the conversation going to be about in terms of where there is to go?" The answer: No place! There is no place to go or get to. This is it. We're here. We've already made it. We've always made it. We have nothing to prove. We can't prove what has always been the truth. Marianne Williamson said so beautifully: "We are brilliant, gorgeous, talented and fabulous. We are the children of God. We were born to make manifest the glory of God that is within us. It's not just in some of us; it's in everyone. And as we let our own light shine, we unconsciously give other people permission to do the same. As we are liberated from our own fears, our presence automatically liberates others."

Next, "Who is this conscious human being going to be interested in?" Other people! Once people handle themselves, once people realize that they are okay and that there's no place to go or get to, they naturally turn their attention to the contribution they can make to others. This was, for me, one of the most profound realizations that occurred as a result of doing the work this book discusses.

It's clear to me, in hindsight, that I spent most of my life with my attention on *me*, concerned with *my* survival, trying to get for *me* what I thought would make *me* happy. It never worked, except for my ego. For the most part, I was unhappy because no matter what I got it was never enough. What I didn't notice, until one of my coaches pointed it out to me, is that I left a long list of hurt, angry and disempowered people in my wake.

Once I "handled" me, got that I was OK, and started putting my attention on what I could do for others, life, true life, began. I have never experienced while trying to do for me, the joy and satisfaction I receive from seeing what I can do for another. This is one of the great paradoxes of life: As long as you're in life for what's in it for you, there's nothing in it for you. It's only when you are in life on behalf of what you can do for others that all of life's riches become available to you.

Finally, "What's this conscious human being going to be up to?" Lots of things, such as having fun; identifying talents, abilities and interests; and figuring out a way he or she can use those talents, abilities and interests to contribute in some way to others and life on our planet.

Every human being has something unique to offer, some gift to give, some contribution to make. When we stop the effort and struggle of "trying to make it" and when we stop being concerned with our survival, we become free to pursue our gifts. When we learn to come from trust and abundance, we stop working just to make a living and start pursuing our passions.

This is a good time to ask yourself: "Are you doing what you're doing because you're passionate about it, or is it a job, something you fell into, something you're doing because you make good money doing it?"

The Path to My Passion

In the 1990s I worked almost exclusively with lawyers and law firms. It's amazing how many lawyers admitted they were lawyers only because they didn't know what else to do with their lives and it seemed like a way to make a good living.

I spoke to many others who were in touch with their gift and who knew what they were passionate about, but they were afraid to leave their law practice because they didn't think they could make enough money doing what they really wanted to do.

If you want to be a new paradigm leader, don't be like those lawyers. You won't win and the people around you won't win either. Here's an important and almost unknown reality: you earn a specific amount of money not because of what you do, but because of where you have evolved to on the scarcity/abundance continuum.

In other words, you "make money" not with your labor, but with your mind. And you take your mindset with you wherever you go. So if you are making $200,000 doing one job, and you quit that job to pursue something you are more passionate about, it won't take long before you are again making $200,000, or more!

This is what happened to me when I retired from practicing law to pursue my new career as a business coach. I had recently joined a large law firm and was two months away from making partner when I decided to retire. I was earning more money than I had ever made before. As a practical matter, I couldn't just walk out the door because I had many clients and lots of responsibilities. I was even managing one of the firms' branch offices.

I made a deal with the firm to phase out over a year. During that year, I turned over my cases and my clients to another lawyer and gradually I disconnected from the firm. In the meantime, I began to pursue what was next, never certain what that might be. I was looking to discover my gift and see where and how to make it available.

This leads me to another of my beliefs. Whenever you commit yourself to something, you are naturally and systematically led in the right direction. W.H. Murray, from The Scottish Himalayan Expedition, summed this belief up best when he said:

> Until one is committed, there is hesitancy, the chance to draw back, always ineffectiveness. Concerning all acts of initiative (and creation), there is one elementary truth, the ignorance of which kills ideas and splendid plans: that the moment one definitely commits oneself, then Providence moves too. All sorts of things occur to help one that would never otherwise have occurred. A whole stream of events issues from the decision, raising in one's favor all manner of unforeseen incidents and meetings and material assistance, which no man could have dreamed would have come his way. I have learned a deep respect for one of Goethe's couplets: *Whatever you can do, or dream you can, begin it. Boldness has genius, power, and magic in it.*

The day I walked out of my law office for good, I still had no idea where I was heading. An almost magical series of events then occurred, none of which I could have imagined or planned. While I did indeed go thirteen months without any income, I was led to the perfect job with the perfect company. Soon I was making more money than I ever did as a lawyer, even though I had neither the formal education nor training to pursue my new profession.

Your Next Step

Continuing with our new design, our conscious human being generates his listening and uses language to create the most empowering and inspiring picture for himself and everyone around him. He generates satisfaction and happiness in his conversation and looks for the gold in everyone he meets.

He neither complains nor gossips, but rather takes action whenever something is not the way he would have it be. He practices "The serenity prayer," popularized by Alcoholics Anonymous:

God, grant me the serenity to accept the things I cannot change, the courage to change the things I can, and the wisdom to know the difference.

Our conscious human being does not withhold her communications, no matter how risky it seems to communicate. Rather, she takes responsibility for her upsets and disappointments and communicates everything appropriately and in a timely manner. Furthermore, when others communicate to her, she listens with compassion, takes responsibility, apologizes and always forgives.

Sound like a daunting task? It is. At least it has been for me. However, it's straightforward and simple, though not necessarily easy. A or B. Is it worth taking on? Absolutely! Is it worth committing yourself and your company to creating an environment where people become conscious human beings supporting each other in that endeavor? Absolutely!

An Example

Remember the company that did development, construction, management and leasing, where it seemed like everyone was making everyone else wrong? I went to the company's office and interviewed everyone. After completing the interviews, I had one of my more interesting conversations with the company president, Mike.

"I have good news and bad news," I began. "The good news is that I have identified the problem. The bad news is that it's you. These people are suffering because they need leadership; they are looking to you to provide it and you're not interested. You're mostly gone, doing your development thing, hoping things will turn out. Well they are not turning out. You're also not very good at acknowledging people and letting them know where they stand with you and some of them feel insecure. You can be negative and sarcastic. You constantly say things that are discouraging."

Imagine how you would feel if someone said that to you. Mike didn't resist what I said at all. In fact, he knew it was the truth. I continued, "People need a leader. Either you're willing to step up and be the leader or we'll have to get someone else. But finding a leader is essential to moving forward."

After a slight pause Mike said, "I'd actually like to take it on. It might be fun. Can you coach me on being the leader?"

"If you're willing, absolutely," I said.

The journey began. First, we took the nine senior executives away for a three-day retreat, talked about everything we've discussed in this book, emptied the files and completed the past.

They all committed to work together to create a future they would all be satisfied with. We distinguished the new paradigm of being human. They all committed to supporting each other in the commitment to become conscious human beings. Then it was time for them to get back to work.

The results were immediate, remarkable and often amazing.

People outside the company frequently complained about one of the women on the team (we'll call her Laura). When others received the complaints, they often agreed with the complainer. The first week back, someone complained about Laura to one of the men on the team who mistrusted her the most. Instead of agreeing with the complainer, he defended Laura and took responsibility for the person's complaint. When I asked him why he did that, he responded that it was time to rehabilitate Laura's reputation in the community, given the commitment she had made.

The team continued its pattern of meeting on a regular basis and the president started consciously acknowledging them for their efforts and accomplishments. Even more significant, when he made a sarcastic remark, someone would immediately tell him to stop. Before long he did.

I continued to speak to the president every week, coaching him on how to most effectively handle difficult situations. I periodically checked in with different team members to see how they and he were doing. Within four months, they were working like a finely tuned machine, enthusiastically supporting each other and keeping their files empty. They all reported that the president was doing a great job as the leader. By the end of six months, my work with the company was done. The president was doing great, the team members were doing great and the company was doing great.

Six months. That's all it took. Admittedly, it was a company of only ninety people. The bigger the company, the longer the process will take, but not proportionately. Once the team at the top starts working together in the new paradigm we have discussed, relationships change throughout the organization. More than two years later, the new paradigm is stronger than ever. The shackles can come off. You can experience the extraordinary!

Summary and Unshackled Leadership Action Items

It is possible to design a new way of operating in the world, a new way of being a human being, a new conversation to live in, which is the antidote to the conversation of the ego. In that conversation:

- You're OK
- There's no place to go or get to
- What you're about is focusing on others
- What you're up to is discovering your talents and abilities and using those talents and abilities to maximize the contribution you make to others.
- You listen with your attention on others
- You generate your satisfaction and happiness
- You practice the serenity prayer
- You do not withhold your communications and you make it safe for others to communicate to you.

1. Go back to the end of Chapter 8 and re-read the last two paragraphs. Start a new document in your computer and title it "My Highest Vision." Take as much time as you need to create a picture, in words, of exactly who you would be if you were living in accordance with your highest and best vision for yourself. Include everything about who you would be, how you would act, what you would do, where you would live, what your relationships would be like, how you would feel, who people would be for you, your place in the world, the contribution you would be making, what your company would be like and a lot more.

2. When you're done carefully read your new document every morning and commit yourself to living that day consistent with your vision.

3. At the end of the day, review the day's events to see how you did. Use each day to learn what you need to work on and work on it.

4. Get yourself a coach.

Chapter 18

The "Partnership" Paradigm: A New Paradigm of Being Related

In addition to our new paradigm for being a human being, which focuses primarily on how we will be and who people will be for us, we also need to design a new paradigm of relating to each other. Lew Epstein used to say that the highest form of human interaction is a "partnership." I believe that a partnership is the only truly satisfying form of interaction. The degree to which people don't operate with each other as "partners" is the degree to which their relationships will be less than satisfactory.

A true partnership relationship is a phenomenon in human interaction. Partnership, when viewed in this manner, provides a context for everyday living and for all of our relationships. If we don't nurture and care for the relationship, it will inevitably die. It is this failure to nurture our relationships that causes the breakup of countless companies every year.

If businesses are to succeed and endure, they must account for the human beings that are bound together in them. A true partnership relationship must include the following elements:

A Shared Vision

Relationships are a shared journey into the future, where each participant contributes what he or she has to offer to the partnership and receives the benefit of what the partnership creates. When people don't think of relationships in this manner, upsets are inevitable.

Recall my definition of a successful enterprise, which is a group of people working together on behalf of a future they have all committed themselves to. For this to be the case, the parties to the relationship need to understand the future or vision they share. Knowing this goes a long way toward ending the bickering that seems so commonplace in personal relationships.

In a business context, a shared vision is frequently missing. It is my suspicion that if you ask the employees in most companies, "What's the company's vision?" the most common answer will be "to make money." And if you ask them, "To make money for whom?" the answer will likely be "for the owners, of course."

Now that wouldn't be a bad thing if making money for somebody else motivated people. It doesn't. Having an inspiring vision that people share is critical to creating a partnership relationship.

When we do the kinds of retreats discussed throughout this book, we make sure people have time to create a shared vision. Not only do people leave the retreat feeling good about themselves and each other, they also leave with a sense of the future they are going to work together to create. This sense of an exciting future helps keep people focused on staying in the new paradigm we have created. They know staying there will be essential to having their shared vision become reality. We will discuss a process for creating such a vision in the next chapter.

Inclusion

We live in an individualistic culture. Our country is the birthplace of the entrepreneur. We are the "rugged individualists." Our folk heroes are John Wayne, the Lone Ranger, Amelia Earhart and now Superman, Batman, and Spiderman.

Entrepreneurs, in particular, are individual decision makers. If a task needs to be done, they make a decision and do it. Could others be adversely affected by the decision? Yes, but the entrepreneur will deal with them later. Right now, someone has to make a decision.

Our entrepreneurial, bottom-line quality is both our strength and our weakness. It works to produce results, but it often doesn't work to build solid and deep relationships, and that's what's missing.

A true partnership operates in a way that is clearly distinct. Its people do not make decisions that affect others without fully discussing the decision with them. When an issue needs resolution, those committed to partnership work to build consensus. They listen to and consider every point of view. They make every possible attempt to reach a conclusion that works for everyone, with no one left out. They always consider other people's feelings and strong points of view.

The above discussion does not preclude the possibility of creating a management team or individual and delegating decision-making authority to that team or individual. In such cases, however, the team or individual must be sensitive to the individual points of view of the others with whom they work. When they need to make a decision, and there is doubt as to whether the decision will be acceptable to all, they must discuss all points of view to ensure a favorable outcome for all. In summary, in a true partnership relationship, decision makers are sensitive to the fact that they are not islands, that their actions impact everyone, and that everyone else's point of view is as important as their own.

This element of partnership is often the biggest source of complaints that we hear from people in companies when we begin a project. "They don't ask me my opinion," "I don't know what's going on," "Some of the things 'they' decide make no sense to me, but do you think 'they' ask me how I feel" are all too frequent comments we hear. Needless to say, these comments are not coming from turned on, motivated, highly productive employees.

I can hear what you are thinking: "This is going to take time. I can't go around and get everyone's opinion and build consensus. I'm too busy to do that." Yes, it will often take time. Do it anyway. You will save much more time in the long run not having to deal with people's upsets because they were not included. You certainly will not have to deal with people attempting to sabotage your plans because they feel left out and unappreciated.

Trust

In the ordinary course of events, people do not trust one another. Every child learns early in life: do not take candy from a stranger; do not talk to strangers; be careful! It is part of our culture to distrust others. So trust becomes something we give carefully. To make matters worse, everyone has been taken advantage of, fooled or duped on a number of occasions.

We believe that trust must be earned after a long period of careful scrutiny. Only after people have performed consistently for an extended period of time can we trust them, and we can do so only as long as they continue to perform. If they stumble, we quickly revoke that trust.

The problem with relating to trust in this manner is that it does not take into consideration the fundamental nature of human beings. The fact is that people are not trustworthy. People are fallible; that is part of being human. No one will consistently perform as promised, keep their word, and do everything they say they will do by when they say they will do it.

This being the case, we can relate to trust in another, more powerful way. We can generate trust by declaration, and stand for it on an ongoing basis. (Remember our discussion about taking a stand.) This is the kind of trust that is essential in a true partnership relationship. People agree to trust one another simply because it is the company's spoken commitment while fully acknowledging that human beings will make mistakes.

When individuals do make a mistake, others can expect that they will acknowledge the mistake and do everything necessary to resolve it. Once resolved, an individual's humanness, or the fact that he or she has messed up, must not cause a revocation of trust. In this scenario, trust is a context for people to work together. It is something generated on an ongoing basis and a place to come from in dealing with the realities of business.

Listening to Each Other

As discussed in Chapters 5 and 15, we need to listen *for the gold* and *with compassion*. This means listening for *possibility* or listening for the other's *commitment*. Whenever possible, it also means listening *and/both* and *win/win*.

When people are upset, it means getting their communication, not getting defensive and always apologizing. In this manner, people can feel safe with each other and true cooperation can result.

Respect for Each Other

Respect is very much like trust. In the ordinary course of events, people earn respect after they have proven their talent and their ability to produce results. Often it's worse than that. People are frequently respected only because they are liked. If an individual is disliked, he or she is discounted and distrusted. This way of dealing with respect is disempowering in a relationship.

In a true partnership it is essential that we generate respect by declaration and stand for it on an ongoing basis. Respect means acknowledging human beings and standing for their worthiness and value. Respect means giving up the right to judge and deciding to give respect based upon commitment rather than upon the results produced. Thus, an individual's humanness and seeming lack of productivity and perfection will not cause a revocation of respect. In this scenario, respect is a context for people to work together. It is something that is generated — a place to come from.

Open and Honest Communication

As discussed in Chapter 15, open and honest communication involves keeping your files empty, taking responsibility for whatever you are experiencing, and talking about everything, openly, honestly and fully.

It also means talking only to the people who are the subjects of whatever communication needs to take place. No complaining about the person and no gossiping to another.

Compassion for Each Other's Feelings

Recently a few specific psychological conversations have become fashionable. The terms "co-dependency" and "dysfunctional family" are on everyone's lips, and people rush to the store to buy John Bradshaw's latest book on healing the inner child.

We need to acknowledge that to some degree everyone is co-dependent and that all individuals come from families that were in some way dysfunctional. In fact, the entire world is dysfunctional. Crime, poverty, drug abuse, war, anger, and violence are everywhere. So within everyone is a sensitive, damaged, and often angry child who grew up in a world where appropriate vehicles to heal the hurts were unavailable. The simple phenomenon of growing up has left people damaged and feeling "not okay."

Despite all of the knowledge available today, appropriate means for dealing with this damage are still not within most people's grasp. So they bring the damage to work and act out in a number of inappropriate ways. People at work neither understand what is going on with an upset individual, nor do they know what to do about inappropriate behavior. We believe we can do little to help and that it is an individual's responsibility to work out his or her own "stuff" single-handedly or with an appropriate professional.

There is, however, something we can do in the office. Faced with another's upset, co-workers can generate compassion, can take the time to listen, can try to understand and appreciate how it must be for the upset individual. Anyone can authentically care that another human being is hurt and upset. A little compassion goes a long, long way to having another feel he or she is not alone in life and that someone else understands and appreciates what he or she is going through.

No Competition

People at work would do well to model their relationships after sports teams, such as professional basketball or football teams. For example, on a football team, everyone plays a different position. Everyone has a different job, and the success of the entire team depends upon everyone doing his job, contributing what he has to contribute.

If basketball players compete with their teammates to gain individual recognition, there is little possibility of the team achieving its goals. Before the Chicago Bulls won their first NBA Championship in the 1990s, Michael Jordon said,

It's hard to celebrate individual accolades with the team and with people, with fans. It's a lot better when you do it as a team, when you become champions as a team. Then everyone can feel some of the excitement that you feel.

And Karl Malone of the Utah Jazz said, in May 1998, after beating the LA Lakers in four straight games in the conference finals,

When you put your minds together as a team, you can accomplish a lot of great things.

Most people do not see the parallel of teamwork in a company. In a company, competition between employees appears to be healthy. It isn't. For one person to win, another must lose and nobody likes losing. When people in a business compete with one another, the partnership's disintegration begins. In a true partnership relationship, everyone understands his or her role and does the very best for the common good. In a true partnership relationship, people win and lose together.

Companies that have large sales staffs often violate this rule with very negative consequences. They have contests and programs that pit each salesperson against the other and then they give awards, prizes, trips, and the like to the one or those who win the contest or produce the greatest result.

Imagine an end-of-year meeting with 50 salespeople where the grand "prize" is given to the top performer. The other 49 applaud politely, trying to be happy for the "winner," but are they really? At the end of the meeting, the reality is that there is one winner and 49 losers.

What about setting up a program where everyone competes against him or herself. Rather than trying to beat the rest of the team, each person's goal for the year is to increase *his or her* performance by some percentage over what *he or she* did the previous year.

Imagine this same group of people at this company's end-of-year meeting. What if 10, 20, 30 or however many people get some bonus, some prize, because they performed at a new level, compared to what *they* did before? In such an environment, people are encouraged to support each other, to work together, because now, in doing so, *everyone* can win! To me this is so obviously more desirable that I'm amazed that companies still have sales competitions that encourage people to sabotage their fellow employees.

No Righteousness

If we were to take life and turn it into a board game, and if the board game could be set up to operate exactly the way human beings operate, then my candidate for the perfect name for the game would be "Be Right." Being right is the greatest human passion. The ego loves it when we are willing to do anything to be right. This need for people to be right shows up every day in every courtroom. It shows up in relationships, between groups of people, between nations, and between political groups. It's everywhere, and it's pervasive.

Not only are individuals *oriented* towards being right, they are also *committed* to being right. Unfortunately, when a person is committed to being right, that person leaves others who have been made wrong in his or her wake. This is why being right and being happy cannot co-exist. It may look as if being right provides happiness, but look again. The happiness is momentary. People are made wrong, relationships are destroyed, and employees fight with each other. In this right/wrong scenario, a partnership relationship is not possible.

A true partnership relationship operates in a distinct way. Team members are willing to give up their positions, their opinions, their firm beliefs, and their need to be right in order to reach consensus, to serve the majority, and to discover what would work best for the whole. They listen to and consider every point of view. They make every possible attempt to reach a consensus with nobody left out. People are more committed to the company's success than to their own passionate positions.

Embracing the Differences

Continuing with the sports analogy, not everyone can be a great quarterback, a great shooting guard or a great shortstop. A football team has room for blockers and tacklers, running backs and receivers. Furthermore, every great quarterback knows that he is nothing without his supporting cast. Sports forces people to recognize and appreciate the differences in their teammates and to include those differences if the team is to be successful.

Unfortunately, most people have not learned this essential lesson. Most people constantly compare others to themselves. They criticize others whenever they don't live up to some set of standards, or they envy them when they've exceeded them. This way of being fosters the right/wrong, good/bad phenomenon discussed previously, leading to envy, jealousy, and antagonism, the forerunners of the disintegration of most relationships.

A workable company has finders, grinders, minders, and binders. Finders bring in the work; grinders do the work; minders manage the company; and binders bring people together. Unfortunately, in our culture, we give more credit to a finder than to the others. But what's the good of finding without those to grind, mind, and bind?

In a true partnership relationship, everyone acknowledges and appreciates other people's contributions and uses each others' talents for the maximum benefit of the team. In a true partnership relationship, it is important that all involved recognize and learn to appreciate who they are and who their teammates are. It is important that they learn to include the differences rather than be irritated by them. When this is done, the differences can provide strength and opportunity to the company.

Does this sound like an exciting way to design our relationships? Yes. And while it sounds simple and straightforward, it's not so easy to do in practice. However, like everything else we've discussed, it's worth taking on. I invite you to do so. You won't be sorry.

Summary and Unshackled Leadership Action Items

In addition to our new paradigm for being a human being, which focuses primarily on how we will be and who people will be for us, we also need to design a new paradigm for relating to each other. A true partnership relationship is a phenomenon in human interaction. Partnership, when viewed in this manner, provides a context for everyday living and for all of our relationships. If we don't nurture and care for the relationship, it will inevitably die. It is this failure to nurture our relationships that causes the breakup of countless companies every year.

1. Go back over the 10 qualities of a partnership relationship and compare them to the reality in your organization. Do you have a shared vision? Do people trust each other? Do people in your organization compete with each other or do they work together as a team, embracing the differences?

2. There's no value in reading this chapter if you're not going to acknowledge and take action on those areas where partnership isn't present. Make a list of all of the areas where you are falling short of having a true partnership.

3. Meet with your management team and come up with a plan of action to bridge the gap between where you are and where you need to be.

I have caught life. I have come down with life. I was a wisp of undifferentiated nothingless, and then a little peephole opened quite suddenly. Light and sound poured in. Voices began to describe me and my surroundings. Nothing they said could be appealed. They said I was a boy named Rudolph Waltz, and that was that. They said the year was 1932, and that was that. They said I was in Midland City, Ohio, and that was that.

They never shut up. Year after year they piled detail upon detail They do it still. You know what they say now? They say the year is 1982, and that I am fifty years old.

Blah blah blah

• Kurt Vonnegut

Chapter 19

Aligning on a Vision for the Future

We're on the home stretch. We've exposed the existing paradigm of being human and being related and designed a new, workable, empowering and inspiring paradigm of being human and being related. Returning to our definition of a successful organization, which is a group of enthusiastic, confident, optimistic, appreciative and happy people who work together on behalf of a future they have all committed themselves to; you can see that the tools for creating the first part of that definition are now clear. The last step is to create a future that everyone can be committed to.

The Scott Hunter Visioning Process

After 23+ years of working with organizations, we have developed a series of questions that help people attain clarity as to the future the company is committed to. Here are the questions:

What Are The Facts Now?

Here the objective is to get clear about what is true right now. Who are you? What does your company look like? Where is it located? What does it do? How many people does it have and serve? What does it look like physically? What are its products or services? Who are its customers? What are its revenues and profits? Write down all the details. Paint a picture of what people would see if they walked into your company today. Stick to the facts.

What Are Your Strengths?

What do you consider your strengths to be? What contributes to the company's success? What do you do well? What are the nice things people say about you? What do you want to maximize?

What Are Your Weaknesses?

What do you consider your weaknesses to be? What gets in the way of the company's success? What could you do better? What are the things people, both internally and externally, complain about? What do you want to minimize?

What Are Your Concerns; What Issues Are You Dealing With?

What do you worry about at night? What doesn't seem to ever get resolved? What is standing in the way of your success? What areas do not seem to be working?

What Is Your Company Vision?

What's your vision for the future? If you had a magic wand and could create anything, what would your company look and feel like? If there were no limitations, if you could steer your company into the future and have anything and everything your heart desired, what would it look like when that happened?

Most companies have, at best, a set of goals and objectives. While it is important for a business to identify its objectives, vision is distinct from a set of objectives. Vision lies in an entirely different realm. It has to do with the nature and kind of business you want to create, the tone and feel of the business for all stakeholders. A vision is inspiring, as in "to land a man on the moon and return him safely" or "to develop a reputation in an industry for providing the highest quality products and the best customer service." A vision is the view of the future that the company is committed to creating. Vision serves to bind people together, as the Declaration of Independence did for our forefathers or as Lee Iacocca's vision for the future did for the employees of Chrysler.

In order to create a company's vision, you must answer several questions:

- What are the fundamental commitments in building this company?
- How would the owners or executives want the company to be so that they could be truly proud of it, happy, and excited about walking into it every morning?
- What are the company's commitments with regard to its customers?

- How would management want their customers to speak about the company? What about the employees?
- How does management want the employees to feel about working at the company?
- How would the owners or executives want to be treated?
- What is the company committed to with regard to the community in which it operates?
- What difference does the company want to make in the lives of its customers, its employees, and its community?
- What is the unique contribution that the company has to make?

Do these questions sound beyond the realm of ordinary conversation? They are but shouldn't be. These exact questions are missing in so many companies, yet they need to be asked if an inspiring vision is to emerge.

What Business Are You In?

This is a basic question. In the days before airplanes, the railroads thought they were in the railroad business. So when air travel came along, they didn't get involved. Yet, had they seen themselves as being in the transportation business, a very different result may have occurred. This is an important question. Exactly what business are you in?

I worked with a group of partners in a firm that took many weeks and many hours of discussion to answer this one question. They knew what business they *had been in,* but they were committed to using that information to advise rather than limit their discussion of what business they would be in in the future.

What Products or Services Do You Offer?

Do you want to be all things to all people or are you limited to a particular set of products and/or services? Successful companies are clear about the products and/or services they offer, and they stick to what they are good at. They have a recognizable brand that people acknowledge and relate to with trust.

To Whom Do You Offer Your Products or Services?

Many successful companies were built because they had a clear picture of their customer. *USA Today* was written for a specific reader. Nordstrom's department store was designed for a specific customer. Many people other than the target market read *USA Today* and shop in Nordstrom's, but both continue to focus on their target customer.

Focus is critical for successful marketing. If you're not clear about whom you are targeting with your products or services, it's like shooting an arrow into a fog and hoping you hit the bulls-eye.

What Is Your Price?

Are you going to compete based on price or on the value you create? Nordstrom's doesn't try to be the cheapest in its field. In fact, it may be more expensive than its competitors. However, many people are willing to pay more given the service they receive. As a coach, I always prided myself on charging *more*, not less, than my competitors. My attitude was that if you wanted the best, and wanted real results, then you'd stop whining about the price and make an investment in your future. If you want to shop for the cheapest, you'll have to go someplace else, but don't complain if you don't get the results you want.

What Is Your Purpose/Mission?

As discussed previously, a powerful mission and an inspiring vision for its future are essential to a company's success. They serve as a source of inspiration for the employees, unleashing their creativity, productivity, and effectiveness. Without such a mission and vision for the future, their work quickly becomes exactly that — work — a dull routine that saps people of their natural aliveness and motivation and leaves them disempowered and resigned.

Although it may have many other names, the mission of an organization is embodied in what is often referred to as its "purpose" or "mission" statement. For example, one of the most successful American companies of our time, Johnson & Johnson, is studied in almost every major MBA program in this country, particularly for its "Credo." Johnson & Johnson's "Credo" is acknowledged throughout its organization as the primary reason for the company's success. As do all well thought-out mission statements, the Johnson & Johnson Credo sets forth the company's fundamental principles and values, and these principles and values will typically include a number of elements.

The first element essential to a clearly stated and effective mission statement responds to the question "What do we do?" The second element addresses the question "What are we committed to in doing what we do?" The third element considers the question "Who are we for our customers or clients?" The fourth element defines "Who are we for our employees/staff?" The fifth element seeks to answer "Who are we for our owners?" And finally, the sixth element is responsive to "Who are we for our community?"

In the case of Johnson & Johnson, the company's key executives consider it their primary purpose to keep the Credo and what it represents in front of every single employee, all of the time. At Johnson & Johnson, the Credo is not merely a collection of noble words. It is something that lives and breathes within every person in the organization.

So what might a mission statement look like? Here is the Johnson & Johnson Credo:

We believe our first responsibility is to the doctors, nurses and patients,
to mothers and all others who use our products and services.
In meeting their needs everything we do must be of high quality.
We must constantly strive to reduce our costs
in order to maintain reasonable prices.
Customers' orders must be serviced promptly and accurately.
Our suppliers and distributors must have an opportunity
to make a fair profit.

We are responsible to our employees,
the men and women who work with us throughout the world.
Everyone must be considered as an individual.
We must respect their dignity and recognize their merit.

They must have a sense of security in their jobs.
Compensation must be fair and adequate,
and working conditions clean, orderly and safe.
Employees must feel free to make suggestions and complaints.
There must be equal opportunity for employment, development and
advancement for those qualified.
We must provide competent management,
and their actions must be just and ethical.

We are responsible to the communities in which we live and work
and to the world community as well.
We must be good citizens — support good works and charities
and bear our fair share of taxes.
We must encourage civic improvements and better health and education.
We must maintain in good order
the property we are privileged to use,
protecting the environment and natural resources.

Our final responsibility is to our stockholders.
Business must make a sound profit.
We must experiment with new ideas.
Research must be carried on, innovative programs developed
and mistakes paid for.
New equipment must be purchased, new facilities provided
and new products launched.
Reserves must be created to provide for adverse times.
When we operate according to these principles,
the stockholders should realize a fair return,

Johnson & Johnson

Long, but impressive.

On a simpler note, the following is an example taken from the real estate development company discussed earlier in Chapter 14:

We are a real estate solutions company. We use our extensive knowledge and experience to provide development, construction, property management, leasing, and/or consulting services to our customers to enable them to maximize the value of their real estate investments.

We know real estate because we own real estate. We listen and present a process that is well thought-out and strategic. We are reliable and trustworthy and act with a high degree of integrity, consistent with our commitment to always exceed the expectations of our customers.

We are a company our employees are proud of. We provide them a fun, exciting, challenging and team-oriented work environment, where they want to come and participate, which encourages and provides opportunities for them to grow personally, professionally and spiritually, and where they are recognized and rewarded for their accomplishments and contributions.

We are committed to maximizing the return on the investment for our customers and owners, that our customers receive value, and that our employees realize their financial goals so that everyone wins out of their participation with our company.

We are good corporate citizens. We give of our time, resources and expertise to worthwhile community organizations; we encourage our employees to participate in community and family activities of their choice and we support them in such activities."

It's immediately apparent that this mission statement includes the six elements discussed previously. Paragraph one sets forth what the company does. Paragraph two sets forth what the company is committed to in doing what it does.

While paragraphs one and two are obviously related, paragraph two sets forth the company's fundamental commitments to its clients. Here the firm commits itself to "listening" and presenting processes that are "well thought-out" and "strategic." They are "reliable," "trustworthy," and operate with "integrity." Its commitment is to always "exceed the expectations of their customers." With the quoted words, the company's mission begins to emerge.

Paragraph three sets forth the company's commitment to its employees. The company is not interested in just any kind of work environment, but only a fun, exciting, challenging and team-oriented work environment, where the employees want to come and participate. It is also clear about the type of opportunities the company is committed to providing its employees.

Paragraph four contains an all-important commitment to the company's ownership. This is a critical element to any organization's purpose, for without profitability, the organization's other objectives will not be fulfilled.

Finally, paragraph five sets forth the firm's commitment to its community. Note that it is up to the employees to identify the areas in which they seek to give back to the community.

If viewed simply as a hollow group of well-intentioned words on a piece of paper, such a mission statement might provoke disdain and skepticism. If the words, even with good intention, were placed on a piece of paper and tucked neatly in a drawer, the document would be worthy of such an attitude.

On the other hand, if the words represent management's deeply felt commitment, if the document is presented to the employees as the company's underlying philosophy, and if the executives and employees alike work together to fulfill the mission, such a written statement will serve as a source of inspiration for the employees, unleashing their creativity, productivity and effectiveness. Such a mission statement can achieve for a company the same motivational effect as Johnson & Johnson's famous Credo, and a company can enjoy the same long-term benefits that such an inspired environment provides.

What Is Your Strategic Vision?

Remember the first question, "What's so?" Now it's time to project five or more years into the future and create a "what's so" for then. Given the strengths, the weaknesses, the vision, the products and/or services, if I walk into the company in five or more years, what will it look like? This becomes the picture that everything is driven towards.

What Are Your Key Objectives For The Next Year?

Now it's time to create three to five key objectives for the next year which, when accomplished, will launch the company powerfully in the direction of its strategic vision. In other words, we're working backwards. Start with the overall vision. From that, create a five-year strategic vision, and then work back to what needs to happen in the next year so that the strategic vision becomes a reality. From this, you can further create objectives for the next quarter, the next month, the next week, and the next day. The key is to work backward from the big picture and the future.

What Is Your Culture?

If the mission, company vision, strategic vision and key objectives set forth the company's philosophy and direction, the culture establishes the "rules of the road." Every company has a culture. Usually, the culture evolves over time. I recommend that you create a culture as an expression of the organization's commitment to the new paradigm discussed in this book.

The organization's culture establishes what behavior is acceptable and expected and what is not. It covers how people are expected to act individually, with each other, with the company's customers and vendors, and with the community in general. A well thought-out culture statement goes a long way toward creating a conscious paradigm. Here's the culture statement created by the real estate development company, whose purpose statement appears earlier in this chapter:

Who we are as a company:

- We are here to serve our customers.
- We recognize and appreciate the uniqueness of each individual and the importance of everyone's contribution to the company. We seek to utilize each person's unique strengths and abilities. No one person is more important than any other.
- We provide all employees opportunities to grow, develop and advance professionally.

- We encourage people to take the initiative to keep up with the industry and their own personal growth and development.
- We maintain a clean, well-organized, comfortable environment. While our atmosphere is casual, dress is appropriate to a professional business environment.
- People's commitments to their moral and/or religious values are never sacrificed.

Who we are as individuals:

- We are our word. We are committed to keeping the promises we make. When we cannot keep our promises, we communicate responsibly.
- We are self-starters; we take initiative and freely and willingly perform our duties at or above the level expected of us.
- While at work, our focus is on the business of the company and we manage our personal lives so that they do not interfere with this focus.
- We are proud of the company and loyal to it.
- We are goal oriented and goal driven. We are accountable for the results we commit to producing.
- We enjoy our work, have a positive attitude and bring fun and enthusiasm to whatever we do.
- We know what work is expected of us and we get our work done completely and on time. We always do the best job we possibly can.
- We do not need the presence of owners, managers or supervisors for the fulfillment of our accountabilities.

- We are punctual in attendance and always deliver a full day's work.
- We're willing to do whatever it takes to get the job done, including being available for overtime when the need arises.
- When our work is completed, we actively look to assist our co-workers.
- We are committed to maximizing efficiency by delegating wherever possible and appropriate.
- We advance in the company by improved performance of duties and by the acceptance of increased responsibilities.
- We are always seeking to increase our knowledge and improve our skills to better enable us to perform our responsibilities.
- We promptly acknowledge our mistakes when they are recognized and immediately act to correct them.
- We do not discuss our pay or benefits with others in the company.
- Our job titles describe job functions and not status.
- We share in the financial and other successes of the company.
- We experience satisfaction and fulfillment out of the company's accomplishments and the benefits derived by the company's customers.
- We use appropriate language in the work environment.
- We do not sabotage the goals or purposes of the company by pursuing an inconsistent personal agenda.
- We are dynamic and talented; we are focused, highly productive and we constantly raise the bar.

Who we are with each other:

- We always communicate openly, honestly, directly and in a timely manner with each other and with our customers. We do not withhold our communications. We are discreet and appropriate when we communicate.
- We do not complain or gossip about each other, the company or our customers. Rather, we express our dissatisfactions and suggestions for improvements and only to someone who can do something about it.
- We operate as a team; operation is seamless to the customer.
- We support each other and take initiative to solve all problems, whether created by us or not.
- We treat each other fairly and with dignity and respect and acknowledge the value of everyone else's work. We do not belittle or abuse other people.
- We care about each other. We treat each other with compassion.
- Our work environment is high energy and fun.
- We rely on each team member to be a key contributor to the objectives of the company; to be responsible and accountable for the commitments they make; and to share their ideas, knowledge, techniques and expertise with the others.
- When we become aware of information relating to a customer, a sale or any other aspect of our business, we promptly share such information with all who have a need to know or will be impacted by the information.

ᨀ We are a team; we win or lose together.

ᨀ We are sensitive to and responsible for the consequences our actions have on others.

ᨀ We value comments and suggestions from all those with whom we work. We express gratitude and appreciation to our co-workers for their efforts.

ᨀ We encourage and support others in the company in their pursuit of worthwhile causes and their personal aspirations.

Who we are with our customers and the community:

ᨀ   We treat everyone we meet as a customer. "Customers" include architects, engineers, vendors, brokers, tenants and everyone else we deal with in doing our jobs.

ᨀ We recognize that how we conduct ourselves in the community reflects on the reputation of the company and we are responsible for our conduct.

ᨀ We greet every customer with a smile.

ᨀ Every contact with a customer is designed to leave them feeling favorably impressed with the level of service they receive.

ᨀ We treat our customers as part of the family.

ᨀ We talk straight with our customers and proactively seek to ensure that they are not misled.

ᨀ We maintain our professional image in our dealings with customers on the telephone and in person. We promptly respond to telephone calls, e-mails, and correspondence.

ᨀ We are creative in our thinking about our customer's needs and look for creative solutions to solve their problems. We're willing to do whatever it takes to make sure the customers' needs are satisfied.

🙠 We honor and respect the confidences of our customers and all matters involving the company.

🙠 We seek opportunities to be actively engaged in good causes and encourage our fellow workers to do the same. The company is willing to financially support employees in community service projects and, whenever possible, we participate as a group in worthwhile community causes.

What Is Your Organizational Structure?

The final step in designing the future is to create an organizational structure that will take you there. Most companies do this by putting all of the people in the organization on a piece of paper and then organizing them in some logical and manageable way. They may also organize the company based on how it exists today. Both approaches only keep the company stuck where it is.

Here's a better approach. Look at your five-year strategic vision. Consider that it has been fulfilled. Now, imagine that none of the people presently in the company are there in five years. Create an organizational structure to efficiently and effectively manage the company as it will be then; no names; just use boxes, functions and titles. Design the most workable management structure you can imagine for that company.

When that's done, and only when that's done, put the people you presently have into the boxes. You will immediately see what's missing in your organization and what will be necessary when you achieve your strategic vision. You will become clear about what will have to happen over the next five years. So pencil in some dates as to when each of the vacant positions will be filled.

When you follow this approach, the organizational structure becomes a road map to fulfilling the strategic vision, and it pulls you into the future you've always known was possible.

Many years ago, a company president and former client invited me to lunch. He said it was a celebration but didn't tell me initially what we were celebrating.

When I arrived at the restaurant he had selected, he started the conversation by saying that I had given him the best advice he had ever received. Not remembering what he was referring to, but being obviously delighted by his comment, I asked what that was.

He said, "you probably don't remember several years ago when we hit $10 million in sales I told you I wanted to be a $25 million company. I had just learned how to run the company at that level and had no clue what it would take for me to get to the next level. You told me to go home and think about what my company would look like when it got to $25 million, completely design that company, and then start acting like the president of the company I designed.

"Well I did exactly that. I first created a picture in my mind of what the company would have to be doing if it's sales were at $25 million, I then created an organizational structure for that company, and then I started acting like that company was already a reality. And why we're celebrating today? We just hit $25 million and it only took a couple of years for that to happen."

Needless to say, I was delighted, not only for him, but because his experience completely validated my advice, which was based on the law of cause and effect. You start thinking consistent with the future you want to create and the universe will send you whatever is necessary to have that become your reality.

The most fun part of the luncheon was the next conversation. After we toasted his success, he said, with a glint in his eye, "I have another question for you. Now I want to be a $50 million company. How do I go about making that happen?" Well before I could open my mouth, he answered his own question by saying, "I know, start acting like the president of a $50 million company."

I was in his neighborhood a couple of weeks ago and not having seen him for quite a while, I stopped by to see how they were doing. He said they were going to hit $82 million this year. By the way, this is the same president discussed earlier whose listening is *win/win/win*. Trust me. This stuff works!

Summary and Unshackled Leadership Action Items

This book's definition of a successful organization is a group of enthusiastic, confident, optimistic, appreciative and happy people who work together on behalf of a future they have all committed themselves to. This chapter sets out a detailed process for creating a future that everyone can commit to.

1. Take time to go through these steps in detail. Do it with your management team and, if possible, with one or more representatives from different parts of your company. It would be wonderful but highly impractical to include everyone.

2. Don't rush through this process. Take your time. We typically take several months to go through all of the questions. While the first few might not take that much time, writing a purpose or mission statement and creating a desirable culture requires a lot of thought and careful consideration.

3. When the design of the future is complete, we highly recommend staging an event to present what you have come up with to your entire company. We have conducted close to one hundred "launching the future" events for our clients and they always serve to create the excitement and enthusiasm that is the hallmark of extraordinary companies.

Chapter 20

Conclusion

We've come to the end of this journey, but your new journey towards becoming a leader and a participant in your new paradigm is just beginning.

Looking back over my years of coaching, I am convinced that the majority of human beings *do* want life to work and want to participate in creating extraordinary success. I can honestly say that I haven't met one mean-spirited, truly nasty person among the tens of thousands we've worked with. Yes, I've met a few with some rough edges, but they all ended up being like the Los Angeles lawyer who got angry all of the time. They had a legitimate commitment but a lousy strategy for fulfilling it. When shown the error of their ways, they were willing to change their strategy and become part of the solution, not the problem.

For you, that's good news. Why? Because no matter how bad your organization's problems may seem, it is unquestionable that the majority of people want the company to succeed and will be your allies in making that happen.

Now it's up to you. You are standing on the doorstep of an incredible opportunity. You have read about processes we have performed hundreds of times with remarkable success. In the past, the only missing pieces were the insights and tools necessary to shift people from the paradigm we inherited to the paradigm that's possible.

What's your choice? At one extreme, you've found this information interesting, possibly enlightening, and maybe even extraordinary. However, if don't act on it, it will slowly but surely fade away — not because that's what you want, but because the "pull" of the existing paradigm is like a rip tide, constantly pulling you under. It's like fishing for crabs. If you put a crab in a big basket, it will crawl out and escape. However, if you put several crabs in the basket and one tries to escape, the others will pull it back in.

As you start on your journey to "the other side," the relentless ego will initially be suspicious and use subtle but effective techniques to sabotage your efforts. If you get good at making the shift, it will get vicious. Don't under estimate its desire to survive.

Therefore, go to the other extreme and take a stand for a new possibility! Commit yourself to a course of action that will allow you to create the paradigm you know is possible. Draw a line in the sand. Gather your key team members and enroll them in this course of action. Most important, create a structure to support you in moving forward.

Take a Stand for Commitment and Support

Most resolutions for change don't work because they are nothing more than good ideas. The person making the resolution has no commitment. Even when he does, he has no support structure. For example, suppose you decide to start jogging three days per week. You are excited and you want to do it, but you have never jogged before.

Your first step is to get a pair of running shoes, shorts and a water bottle. Armed with the right equipment, you decide that tomorrow at 5:30 a.m. you will make your first attempt at jogging. You go to sleep the night before ready for the task. What happens? The alarm goes off at 5:15 a.m. and you are confronted with how dark it is, how cold it is to get out of bed, and how much you want to sleep more. Jogging doesn't seem like such a good idea so you turn off the alarm and go back to sleep. You had no support structure.

If you really want to start jogging, I suggest that you find someone who regularly gets up at 5:15 a.m. three days a week and who commits to making sure you do what you say you will do. He calls you at 5:15 a.m., tells you to get your butt out of bed, and arrives at your home in fifteen minutes to take you running. You agree with him in advance that he will not take no for an answer and that he'll drag you out of bed if necessary so that you keep your commitment. Most important, you build in consequences if you don't keep your end of the deal.

I once had a partner who arrived late to most of our partnership meetings. I told him one day that his tardiness was unacceptable and that there would be consequences if he continued this behavior. He agreed, on his own, to pay me $1 for every minute he was late for a meeting. The first meeting he was late by five minutes and paid me $5. The next meeting he was late by seven minutes and paid $7. I was beginning to hope he would continue being late. However, when he was twenty minutes late to the next meeting and had to pay me $20, he never arrived late again. Consequences work!

You, your team and your company have an enormous opportunity. You can break out of the ordinary, out of business as usual, and create an extraordinary organization. Now you have the guide. I invite you to take a stand, commit, get into action and build a support structure. Ask yourself, "What kind of paradigm do I want to create?" Whatever you want *is* within your reach. Don't expect anyone to hand it to you. Only you can make it happen.

Is such a shift simple? Yes. Is it easy? No. But like the real estate company, the San Francisco law firm, and the hundreds of other organizations that have exerted the effort and committed themselves to this approach, it can become reality.

As you move forward with your new commitment, I wish you the best on your journey. If by chance you should stumble or fall, remember that you can always come back and revisit the conversation here, re-commit, get re-inspired and start again. As you have likely heard so many times before, "life is a journey, not a destination." Enjoy the trip, have fun, and always remember: it's one or the other of just two conversations.

About the Author

Scott Hunter has been transforming organizations for over two decades, through keynote speeches, workshops, retreats and management team coaching.

Since 1985 he has helped hundreds of businesses, delivered over 1,000 speeches and worked with over 100,000 individuals as a business coach and speaker. He has conducted over 150 corporate retreats for groups as small as 2 and as large as 44, consistently producing breakthroughs in the participants personal and professional lives and setting the stage for the companies they manage to achieve results that go way beyond their expectations.

Clients say things like, "In the 9 months since we started to work with you, we've had more opportunities and successes than in the previous 9 years." Or, "You changed the way we do business and oh yes, my family life works better too."

Scott didn't start out as an organizational change agent. Following receipt of an engineering degree from the City University of New York, Scott spent four years working in the U.S. Patent and Trademark Office in Washington, DC while he attended George Washington Law School at night, graduating in the top 10% of his class. He moved to California and eventually opened a private law practice.

Scott's own success journey seemed to be stalled. After 11 years, he was still struggling to pay the bills. He was divorced. Even his secretary quit.

And that's when Scott's real career started. He began researching what it takes for people to produce extraordinary results in their personal lives and careers and for companies to break through to new levels of profitability and success. He took classes. He read books and signed up for one seminar after another.

It took several years, but ultimately Scott's whole life turned around. He became a partner in a major law firm, managing an office and enjoying an income he had only dreamed of previously.

In 1983, Scott decided to retire from his law practice so he could help other companies make the same success journey he had made. Using what he learned painfully, through trial and error, he realized he could guide others to move to their own success goals, bypassing costly, time-consuming detours. He created a 5-step system to deliver repeatable results and he has been teaching that system for the last 20+ years.

Now Scott works as a successful business coach and speaker. He speaks to thousands of people each year and shares advice with CEOs of corporations of all sizes. His book, *Making Work Work* has received successful reviews and garnered a following among executives, professionals and students. He's been recognized as an "expert" on over 50 radio talk shows and appeared on a number of television news programs. And he makes time for his favorite avocation: cycling trips to explore new countries and scenes around the world.

Scott continues to work to stretch the limits of his knowledge and his capabilities. He has spent hundreds of thousands of dollars and devoted months of his life to seminars and programs. He's studied with the best coaches, motivational speakers and industry leaders.

"Scott has the rare ability to touch people's hearts and turn those emotions into practical action; to rattle cages and challenge the status quo, then provide a roadmap for audiences to follow; to discuss broad life values and connect them to work-related values."

to order
multiple copies of

Unshackled Leadership

at a discount

call 1-877-237-0207

or order on-line at:
www.unshackledleadership.com

For information about our
coaching, retreats, programs, seminars or workshops,
contact

THE HUNTER PARTNERSHIP ALLIANCE
Irvine, California
Toll free: 877-237-0207 • Phone: 714-573-8855
Fax: 714-573-8860
Visit our company web site: www.thpalliance.com
Or send us an e-mail: info@thpalliance.com

For information about booking
Scott Hunter as a speaker
Call the numbers above
Or visit our web site: www.scotthunter.com
Or send Scott an e-mail: Scott@scotthunter.com

Free on the web
• Articles on Teamwork, Relationships, Communication
• Self-Assessment Questionnaire

Sign up for our free monthly Electronic Newsletter
"The Coach's Corner"
Sign up information is on both of the above web sites

Hunter Alliance Press